Prologue

As American's we like to believe the justice system applies to all equally. It doesn't. Some crimes are specifically created to impact the poor such as vagrancy, loitering, public intoxication, trespassing on public land and curfews. The poor have limited access to lawyers, and public defenders may spend less than 5 minutes familiarizing themselves with a case before representing it in court.

Crimes that apply to the wealthy, or white-collar crimes, are less likely to be reported and only a small percent of those are prosecuted. The wealthy can afford hefty fines to avoid prosecution. They can afford experienced lawyers who know all the nuances of the law. Prosecution of high-profile individuals is usually proceeded by public outcry and exposure of the inequity of the justice system in prosecuting wealthy or powerful people.

It is obvious to many of us that Hillary Clinton and her family have committed crimes. We expect Attorney General Sessions to follow through on his duties and prosecute her. We may have accepted Donald Trump's campaign rallying cry to lock her up as a promise. The truth is the President cannot compel prosecution and the Attorney General has many considerations before deciding to prosecute a case and ample allowed time to do so.

As frustrating as this may be, there are reasons she has yet to be prosecuted. The unequal treatment of people based upon socio-economic factors is real, but only a small part of why Hillary Clinton has not been prosecuted.

Since the 15th century, Lady Justice has often been depicted wearing a blindfold. The blindfold represents

objectivity, in that justice is or should be meted out objectively, without fear or favor, regardless of money, wealth, fame, power, or identity; blind justice and impartiality.

Perhaps it is the public who are blinded by this notion. Perhaps it is willful thinking that wealthy or powerful people are treated the same under the law. In truth the law favors the wealthy at every stage.

Certain crimes only pertain to the poor. vagrancy, loitering, public urination, and to an extent trespassing are laws designed to impact the poorest people in our society.

Lack of insurance, car tabs and possession of a valid driver's license unfairly impact the poor. A poor person will have their car impounded if they do not have insurance A wealthy person can claim they are self-insured and not even get a ticket. Wealthy people often do not drive themselves, reducing the risk of any road related incidents from occurring.

Child abuse occurs across the socio-economic spectrum, but it is most commonly noted amongst the poor. The rich are more isolate by large estates with hedges and walls. Children are tutored or attend private schools. They are often cared for by nannies. The isolation of the rich makes it more difficult to identify child abuse. Options such as obtaining high price treatment, paying off victims, or having powerful attorneys negotiate deals out of court are common. Poor are more likely to live near others. Children attend public schools. Lack of money for food or proper clothing can be misinterpreted as abuse when it is truly a sign of poverty.

Insider trading may hit the wealthy more often than the poor. Usually this is an issue that is resolved through negotiated settlements and sometimes an agreement that the accused not be allowed to trade for a period. In rare cases, like Martha Stewart, there will be jail time at facilities that may or may not resemble a jail. Insider trading law does not apply to all.

Congress members are exempt from insider trading laws. Although they are the very ones who pass the laws which impact the stock market, they exempted themselves from these laws.

For the most serious crimes of murder and assault, the wealthy are in a much better position to be acquitted because they can afford to hire the best criminal lawyers to defend themselves. These lawyers are better equipped than public defenders to raise a reasonable doubt in the eyes of the court.

Money, power, and influence do play a role in why Hillary Clinton is not in jail. It is actually a minor factor compared to the others, but is the one the general population focuses most on.

We live in a divided country. Those on the political right believe what they believe and there is little a liberal can do to change that opinion. Those on the political left are equally entrenched in their own opinions. If Hillary were to be prosecuted tor convicted there would certainly be civil unrest which would make those disruptions that occurred after the election pale in comparison. The unrest could absolutely result in civil war if those on the right become fed up with the liberal antics and engage them on the streets.

The logical way prosecute Clinton is to wait until Hillary falls from grace of the democratic party and her followers. The liberal media must demonstrate that they erred in their support of Clinton and begin reporting truth. There is motion in both arenas. Elizabeth Warren and Donna Brazile have both taken steps away from the failed presidential candidate. Pelosi, Waters and Schumer have suddenly gone silent. Many are finding Hillary a liability rather than an asset for the democratic party. The party must distance itself from being identified with corruption prior to the 2018 elections. If she is to be held accountable for her crimes, the clarion call must come from the democrats themselves. This is quite possible since she hijacked the DNC and rigged the primaries and plenty of people on the left arc angry about that.

Successful prosecution requires solid evidence. The evidence required to prosecute Clinton would likely involve classified and top-secret documents being presented to the court. If the necessary documents are not provided there will not be enough evidence to prove that she broke the law. If the documents are released the protection of classified material will be compromised for this case and set a precedent for future cases to obtain material normally protected for national security reasons. Judges, lawyers, and clients who do not have clearance to view these documents, would be required to do so if they are entered into evidence.

Releasing confidential material can impact the stability of other countries. Reflecting back to the first wiki-leaks release, that occurred while Clinton was Secretary of State, many allied countries were shown in a bad light. The information led to the start of the Arab spring uprisings. Documents are kept top secret for many reasons, usually because they include material that can harm our government or those of others throughout the world.

Hillary Clinton knows secrets about very powerful people who could be embarrassed through testimony in court. She has had access to 5 Presidents. When Bill Clinton was elected and announced Hillary as co-President and gave her a position as an adviser, she had access to him constantly. She knows his secrets. George Bush Senior, offered his assistance to his successor. Bill Clinton took him up on that offer and they became close friends. George and Barbara Bush said they thought of him as a son. They were less fond of Hillary, but she did have access to the ex-President and likely some secrets related to Bush Seniors administration. When Bill Clinton's term ended he offered his assistance to George W. Bush. Bush Junior accepted the offer and they too became close friends. George W. Bush referred to Bill Clinton as being his brother. He was less fond of Hillary, but she had access to him personally as well as through her new role as Senator. She likely knows some of his secrets. Despite her damning comments against Obama during the Presidential primary, she joined his cabinet. The two were forced to work closely together on many projects. She likely knows some of his secrets and is undoubtedly complicit in some of them as well.

As a businessman, President Trump donated to many candidates on both sides, including Hillary Clinton's campaign against Obama. Trumps condition for the donation was that she attend his wedding, which she did. She claimed she went because she thought it might be fun, but she was paid to attend through the campaign donation.

There likely is not much connection between the two, but it's possible Hillary knows some secrets about Trump as well.

If she were put on trial, there would be great risk that she might either purposefully or negligently expose some Presidential secrets.

If information leaks about our former Presidents, our government officials or shady deals that were made on their behalf, the integrity of the entire government may come into question. When people lose faith in the government and its institution, anarchy reigns.

Loss of confidence in the government can jeopardize the treaties, agreements, and deals we already have in place with other countries. If we back away from international agreements, we risk becoming untrustworthy in international diplomacy matters.

We are in a tenuous position with regards to North Korea. If diplomatic options fail, it is possible the war to follow will be devastating for many. It will also likely rally the left in opposition as evidences by protests against past military actions. Pursuing charges against Hillary Clinton at this time would further divide our country and potentially force our military to be fighting a war at home as well as abroad.

Globalists and the deep state are motivated towards actions that would create a global government, or new world order. Their goals are not necessarily in the best interest of the United States. They have been successful in providing funding for organizations that create chaos and disruption. They are upset that our elected President, unlike the past 4, is a nationalist not a globalist. The Trump administration acting against Clinton while replacing globalist inspired legislation would enhance the likelihood of bankrolled violence in our cities and a greater risk for assassination of our public officials.

America is the world's de facto leader. Others watch what we do. Jailing political opponents is something most of the world equates with under-developed countries, ruled by despots. Despite ample reasons to arrest Hillary Clinton, the world perception would be that she is being persecuted as a Political Prisoner, rather than a citizen atoning for her crimes.

The only way she will be prosecuted is through a steady erosion of her public persona, a dedication to fair reporting by all establishment media and a commitment by liberal politicians to purge their negative public image by sacrificing Clinton and demanding prosecution.

THE DIVIDED STATES OF AMERICA

We must accept that our country is divided. Despite Donald Trump's obvious win in the election, people on the left have remained unsettled. Protests have developed into violence, looting, crime, and rioting. Well financed, opposition groups appeared to disrupt progress of our nation.

Had Clinton won the election, it is unlikely the political right would have accepted the election and supported her as President either. In reality, this past election was bi-polar with most people either hating or loving their candidate, with a miniscule minority who voted for third party candidates in protest. It is likely a portion of the right would have protested and obstructed her Presidency.

We are divided, at least politically. Prosecuting Clinton would make her a martyr for leftists. The likelihood that those on the left would lose their collective minds, especially if she were to be convicted is very high. Patience on the right is being stretched to the breaking point as protesting liberals attack our cities and institutions. The possibility that these tensions could turn into a civil war, is much higher than we may be willing to admit. Should such a war begin it would be a war without defined boundaries; one in which violence could occur anywhere at any moment.

As Clinton's crimes go unpunished, the right is collectively building in frustration. If she does not get held accountable for breaking the law, then why should anybody be held accountable for their crimes? The potential for anarchy exists on both sides, although the left is actively putting it into practice.

(Portland Oregon Election Riots)

Police in Portland, Oregon declared that a once peaceful protest was a riot after demonstrators were seen attacking drivers and committing acts of vandalism during their march against Donald Trump's election.

Portland police said at least 29 people were arrested in the riot. One driver had her windshield smashed and someone painted "Capitalism kills" on a nearby convenience store. Police declared the protest a riot.

The state Department of Transportation briefly shut down Interstate 5 between the Marquan Bridge and the Fremont Bridge due to the demonstration. Parts of Interstate 84 were also temporarily closed.

Protesters in Portland's Pearl District were breaking windows of several businesses and some were arming themselves with rocks.

(Oakland Election Rioting)

Violence erupted in the Bay Area after the election. During protests against Donald Trump's historic presidential victory, unrest in the Bay rea spread quickly.

Protesters set trash cans on fire, and vandalized several businesses, and shattered store fronts on Broadway. A Wells Fargo Bank between 12th and 13th Streets was vandalized. Several hundred protesters shouted anti-trump chants and scrawled graffiti.

Another group of demonstrators tried to block Highway 24. During the demonstration, a female protester was hit by a car and suffered major injuries. The driver stayed at the scene and cooperated with CHP investigators despite protesters attacking her car and smashing her windows. There were about 200 demonstrators on the highway to the onramp.

(Costa Mesa Election Riots)

Protests turned violent prior to the election as well. Hundreds of demonstrators filled the street outside the Orange County amphitheater where Donald Trump held a rally, stomping on cars, hurling rocks at motorists and forcefully declaring their opposition to the Republican presidential candidate.

Traffic came to a halt as a crowd walked in the roadway. Protesters smashed a window on at least one police cruiser, punctured the tires of a police sport utility vehicle, and at one point tried to flip a police car.

One Costa Mesa police officer was struck in the head by a rock thrown by a protestor, authorities said. The officer wasn't injured because he was protected from by his riot helmet.

About five police cars were damaged in total, police said, adding that some will require thousands of dollars' worth of repairs.

(Seattle Election Riots)

At least five people were wounded after gunfire rang out nearby an anti-Donald Trump protest in Seattle.

Hundreds of demonstrators outraged over the outcome of the election were moving through the city's downtown area toward Capitol Hill when gunfire erupted.

A male victim was transported to an area hospital with critical injuries after the shooting. The other four were treated for serious, but not life-threatening injuries.

(Los Angeles Election Riots)

Thousands of people poured into the streets of downtown Los Angeles, and hundreds of them later spilled onto the 101 Freeway, shutting down traffic as they forcefully denounced President-elect Donald Trump.

The 101 Freeway, a key thoroughfare in metropolitan Los Angeles, reopened after 4 a.m. once debris was cleaned up.

In the loud and aggressive demonstration, many chanted, not my president. The mostly young crowd marched through the city before heading onto the freeway near Alameda Street.

The pack of hundreds, many screaming against both Trump and law enforcement, others riding skateboards on the freeway, caused a traffic backup that extended for miles. At least 13 people were arrested.

The left is angry and still in shock a year after the election. They anticipated the coronation of Clinton was inevitable. The Trump landslide that occurred was not something they had remotely considered.

The media fortified the belief that she was unbeatable. People spoke only with likeminded individuals and ostracized those with differing beliefs. The liberals had created a bubble within which they only heard their own opinions.

Leftist violence is not limited to rioting. After the election, twitter and other social media were flooded with calls for President Trump's assassination as well as that of conservative media reporters, conservative officials and any Trump supporter.

According to Shear, Michael, et al. June 14, 2017, *A lone gunman who was said to be distraught over President Trump's election opened fire on members of the Republican congressional baseball team at a practice field in this Washington suburb using a rifle to shower the field with bullets that struck four people, including Steve Scalise, the majority whip of the House of Representatives.*

Law enforcement authorities identified him as James T. Hodgkinson, 66, from Belleville, Ill., a suburb of St. Louis. His social media accounts show he was a staunch supporter of Bernie Sanders.

Standing at second base, Mr. Scalise was struck once in the left hip, according to witnesses, and collapsed as the shots rang out, one after another. His injuries were extensive, and he was in critical condition

"Just left hospital," Mr. Trump tweeted. "Rep. Steve Scalise, one of the truly great people, is in very tough shape - but he is a real fighter. Pray for Steve!"

Senator Rand Paul of Kentucky, who was among the lawmakers practicing for the annual charity baseball game, told CNN that "the field was basically a killing field, it's really sick and very sad."

As the magnitude of the episode became apparent, House leaders canceled the day's votes, and Mr. Trump and Vice President Mike Pence canceled speeches. Mr. Hodgkinson seemed to be a fervent opponent of Mr. Trump. He signed an online petition calling for the president to be impeached.

His brother, Michael Hodgkinson, said Mr. Hodgkinson traveled in recent weeks to Washington to protest. "I know he wasn't happy with the way things were going, the election results and stuff,"

Mr. Hodgkinson also appeared to have been a fervent fan of Senator Bernie Sanders, according to a Facebook page with references to the Vermont senator. A LinkedIn page for James Hodgkinson had a profile photo showing Mr. Sanders's famous hair and glasses and the words, "The Dawn of a New Democracy."

Mr. Williams, of Texas, praised the two officers as "heroes," saying that their split-second decision to confront the gunman saved many lives. We saw two people risk their lives to save others; we saw courage in the face of death," Mr. Williams said in a news conference Wednesday evening. "There could have easily been 25 deaths or more today."

If there is a high-profile activity occurring, such as a
congressional softball game, we can anticipate (at least in
hindsight) that it could pose risks to the participants and
add security to future events. If a controversial ruling is
about to be made in court, we can anticipate at least
localized civil unrest and bring in additional security.
Random acts of violence are more difficult to predict or
diffuse.

According to Greenwood, Max, 2017, *Kentucky State
Police have arrested a man accused of assaulting
Sen. Rand Paul at his home in Bowling Green.*

*"Senator Paul was blindsided and the victim of an
assault," Kelsey Cooper, a spokeswoman for Paul,
said in a statement. "The assailant was arrested, and
it is now a matter for the police."*

*The suspect was identified as 59-year-old Rene
Boucher of Bowling Green, according to a statement
from police. The Warren County Attorney's Office
issued a warrant for Boucher's arrest shortly after
the assault on Friday.*

*Police are investigating the assault, according to the
statement. Boucher has been charged with 4th degree
assault.*

Rand suffered 5 broken ribs and damage to his
lungs. Boucher was a Bernie Sanders supporter.

There is little doubt in the minds of many that
Hillary Clinton has broken the law on more than one
occasion. After the President has been in office for a year,
protesters still create chaos in major cities. Clinton and
Sanders supporters have not abandoned their respective

candidates. By holding Clinton accountable for her crimes, the left would brand it as persecution of a political rival and Hillary would become their martyr. We must be willing to accept that there will be civil unrest in most major cities around the country, likely including riots and death of innocents. A good frame of reference would be the loss during the Rodney King riots in South Central Los Angeles. After 5 days of rioting, 63 people were dead, over 4000 people were injured and over a billion dollars of damage occurred to the city. The rioting was limited to a small area of Los Angeles. Imagine the devastation of the event if it were going on in all major cities across the country at once.

It is essential that any prosecution of Hillary Clinton occur once her crimes have been exposed and accepted by the left. The left must be the ones to insist on prosecution. In the end, much of the actual damage was caused to the DNC and politicians who had at one time given unwavering support to Clinton.

Currently Warren, Brazile and DNC Chair Perez have taken the bold step to admit Clinton rigged the DNC primary. These are top supporters who had the ability to know what really happened. They need to rebuild some credibility within the democratic party before the 2018 elections. Policing their own is one way to establish credibility. When attacked the Clinton's will try to impeach the credibility of their accusers. Brazile has, in recent days, had her credibility challenged by Clinton, Obama and their minions. They do not seem happy about her truthful revelations.

Pelosi and Waters have inexplicably, yet blessedly, gone silent. Even Anderson Cooper, CNN's liberal Clinton supporter grilled former Clinton campaign manager, Robby Mooks over Clintons involvement in obtaining the Russian dossier.

The left is beginning to turn on the mighty Clinton's.

<u>THE IMPACT ON NOT LOCKING HER UP</u>

Unless the radical elements on the left are pacified by over Democratic leaders we should anticipate civil unrest and rioting the likes of which we have never seen. Based upon the damage and casualties incurred during the Rodney King riots, the property damage could be in the 100's of billions of dollars, disruption of the workforce and loss of tourism and productivity could increase that number into the trillions. Deaths would be in the thousands and injuries in the tens of thousands.

Avoiding this tragedy will require patience and proper timing. The imaginary legacy of Clinton must be degraded over a period of time and her true crime and corruption exposed. The radical elements of the left must be diffused.

BEYOND THE ARAB SPRING

Secrets held by our government are sometimes kept to protect our country. Sometimes those secrets are kept to protect other governments. National security demands that these documents be protected.

One of the main concerns about Hillary Clinton's use of a private server to house government e-mails was that the e-mails did not have the ability to protect national security secrets. The other concern was that the private server situation allowed Clinton to function outside of the public view, avoiding Freedom of Information Act requests, and the leaving of an incomplete and selective public record for the future.

If Hillary Clinton were to be charged with mishandling confidential material, there is ample evidence that would support the charge. Getting a conviction would be more difficult. Technically, with a few exceptions, the designation of security level on intergovernmental correspondence is decided by the person in charge of the Department where the correspondence originated. In the case of the State Department at the time, that person was Hillary Clinton. She could simply claim that she, as Secretary of State, designated them as not confidential. In order to dispute this, the government prosecutors would need to be allowed to enter top secret information into evidence, some of which even the judges might not be qualified to examine. She could also deflect that any information sent to her by other departments and designated as confidential of higher was not solicited by her and that blame falls upon the sender. The exception would be any information that discusses foreign governments which is automatically designated as top secret.

Ironically, democrats will argue that Hillary Clinton's use of a private server did not jeopardize national security while at the same time pushing a false narrative that a foreign government hacked their DNC computers. Evidence currently suggests that the DNC computers were not hacked, but that someone within the DNC downloaded the information on a portable drive. Speculation has often been that the someone was the late Seth Rich.

In general, e-mail is not a secure way to transmit secure information. It is for this reason companies still use faxes for delivering more secure information. It is for this reason that government agencies develop internal e-mail systems that can offer the additional security necessary to protect documents during transmission, delivery, and storage.

(Julian Assange)

The danger of communication intercepts about other governments and our operatives abroad became apparent in 2010 when Julian Assange released diplomatic cables through his Wikileaks web site.

According to Anderson, Lisa, 2011, *Former Tunisian President Zine elAbidine Ben Ali-the first Arab dictator to fall to mass protests-initially seemed an unlikely victim. Tunisia has long enjoyed the Arab world's best educational system, largest middle class, and strongest organized labor movement. Yet behind those achievements, Ben Ali's government tightly restricted free expression and political parties. In an almost Orwellian way, he cultivated and manipulated the country's international image as a modern, technocratic regime and a tourist-friendly travel destination.*

Beyond the cosmopolitan facade frequented by tourists lay bleak, dusty roads and miserable prospects. It is small wonder that the Islamists' claim that the government was prostituting the country for foreign exchange resonated in Tunisia. Ben Ali's family was also unusually personalist and predatory in its corruption. As the whistleblower Web site WikiLeaks recently revealed, the U.S. ambassador to Tunisia reported in 2006 that more than half of Tunisia's commercial elites were personally related to Ben Ali through his three adult children, seven siblings, and second wife's ten brothers and sisters. This network became known in Tunisia as "the Family." That said, although the scale of corruption at the top was breathtaking, Ben Ali's administration did not depend on the kind of accumulation of small bribes that subverted bureaucracies elsewhere, including in Libya and, to a lesser extent, Egypt. This means that Tunisia's government institutions were relatively healthy, raising the prospects for a clean, efficient, and technocratic government to replace Ben Ali. Tunisia's military also played a less significant role in the country's revolt than the armed forces in the other nations experiencing unrest. Unlike militaries elsewhere in the Arab world, such as Egypt, the Tunisian army has never experienced combat and does not dominate the domestic economy. Under Ben Ali, it existed in the shadow of the country's domestic security services, from which Ben Ali, a former military police officer, hailed. Although its refusal to support Ben Ali's regime contributed to the country's revolution, the military has not participated meaningfully in managing the transition period and is unlikely to shape the ultimate outcome in any significant way.

(Zine elAbidine Ben Ali)

The events in Tunisia set of the Arab Spring of revolts throughout the Arab world. The communication seemed fairly innocuous stating half of the countries corporations were headed by people related to the ruler. The information was enough to overthrow the government. The U.S. needs allies both large and small. Their information is protected as are our secrets. It is for this reason that anything related to foreign governments is automatically considered confidential.

Cables are considered much more secure than e-mails but they were still intercepted or leaked. The release of this information had an impact beyond the Arab Spring. Wikileaks exposed our spy network in China.

According to Jones, Ed, 2017, *Beijing systematically dismantled CIA spying efforts in China beginning in 2010, killing or jailing more than a dozen covert sources, in a deep setback to US intelligence there. 10 current and former American officials who spoke on condition of anonymity, described the intelligence breach as one of the worst in decades.*

Of the damage inflicted on what had been one of the most productive US spy networks, however, there was no doubt: at least a dozen CIA sources were killed between late 2010 and the end of 2012, including one who was shot in front of colleagues in a clear warning to anyone else who might be spying.

In all, 18 to 20 CIA sources in China were either killed or imprisoned. It was a grave setback to a network that, up to then, had been working at its highest level in years. Western espionage services have traditionally found it exceptionally hard to develop spy networks in China and Russia.

The CIA's mole hunt in China, following the severe losses to its network there, was intense and urgent. Nearly every employee of the US Embassy in Beijing was scrutinized at one point, the newspaper said.

Meantime, then-president Barack Obama's administration was demanding to know why its flow of intelligence from China had slowed. The revelations come as the CIA seeks to determine how some of its highly sensitive documents were released two months ago by WikiLeaks, and the FBI examines possible links between the Donald Trump campaign and Russia.

It was later determined the leaked information came from Bradley Manning (AKA Chelsea Manning). The damage to trust between nations and the United States was severely impacted by the revelations made through Wikileaks. That trust is still being rebuilt.

(Bradley Manning)

According to Leigh, David, 2010, *The United States was catapulted into a worldwide diplomatic crisis due to the exposure of more than 250,000 classified cables from its embassies.*

The initial revelations disclosed that Arab leaders privately urged an air strike on Iran and that US officials have been instructed to spy on the UN leadership. These two revelations alone would be likely to reverberate around the world. But the secret dispatches, which were obtained by WikiLeaks, revealed Washington's evaluation of many other highly sensitive international issues.

They identified a shift in relations between China and North Korea, high-level concerns over Pakistan's growing instability, and details of clandestine US efforts to combat al-Qaida in Yemen.

Among scores of disclosures the cables detailed:

• Grave fears in Washington and London over the security of Pakistan's nuclear weapons program, with officials warning that as the country faces economic collapse, government employees could smuggle out enough nuclear material for terrorists to build a bomb.

• Inappropriate remarks by Prince Andrew about a UK law enforcement agency and a foreign country.

• Suspicions of corruption in the Afghan government, with one cable alleging that vice-president Zia Massoud was carrying $52m in cash when he was stopped during a visit to the United Arab Emirates.

• Allegations that Russia and its intelligence agencies are using mafia bosses to carry out criminal operations, with one cable reporting that the relationship is so close that the country has become a "virtual mafia state".

• The extraordinarily close relationship between Vladimir Putin, the Russian prime minister, and Silvio Berlusconi, the Italian prime minister, which caused intense US suspicion. Cables detailed allegations of lavish gifts and lucrative energy contracts.

• Devastating criticism of the UK's military operations in Afghanistan by US commanders and the Afghan President.

The US has particularly intimate dealings with Britain, and some of the dispatches from the London embassy range from political criticisms of David Cameron to requests for specific intelligence about individual MPs.

The cables contain specific allegations of corruption, from Caribbean islands to China and Russia. The material includes a reference to Putin as an "alpha-dog" and Hamid Karzai as being "driven by paranoia", while Angela Merkel allegedly "avoids risk and is rarely creative". There is also a comparison between Mahmoud Ahmadinejad and Adolf Hitler.

The cables name Saudi donors as the biggest financiers of terror groups, and provide an extraordinarily detailed account of an agreement between Washington and Yemen to cover up the use of US planes to bomb al-Qaida targets. One cable records that Yemeni President Abdullah Saleh said: "We'll continue saying they are our bombs, not yours."

Other revelations include a description of a near "environmental disaster" last year over a rogue shipment of enriched uranium, technical details of secret US-Russian nuclear missile negotiations in Geneva, and a profile of Libya's Muammar Gaddafi.

(Muammar Gaddafi)

Clinton led a frantic damage limitation exercise as Washington prepared foreign governments for the revelations, contacting leaders in Germany, Saudi Arabia, the Gulf, France and Afghanistan.

US ambassadors in other capitals were instructed to brief their hosts in advance of the release of unflattering pen-portraits or nakedly frank accounts

29

of transactions with the US which they had thought would be kept quiet.

The cables published reveal how the US uses its embassies as part of a global espionage network, with diplomats tasked to obtain not just information from the people they meet, but personal details, such as frequent flyer numbers, credit card details and even DNA material. Classified human intelligence directives instruct officials to gather information on military installations, weapons markings, vehicle details of political leaders as well as iris scans, fingerprints, and DNA.

Washington now faces a difficult task in convincing contacts around the world that any future conversations will remain confidential.

<u>THE IMPACT ON NOT LOCKING HER UP</u>

The international community would be nervously watching any case involving Hillary Clinton. As Secretary of State, the kind of messages disclosed in the Wikileaks cables are the same kind Clinton would have handled daily.

In all likelihood, if Clinton were to be put on trial, she would plead the 5th, or if she wanted to appear cooperative she would use her well-rehearsed, "I do no recall" mantra

Prosecution would require the introduction of evidence in the form of documentation. The Trump administration would likely face significant pressure from other governments not to prosecute Clinton based upon their own national security interests.

As we are faced with a decision whether to use diplomatic or military options with North Korea, it is essential that our allies and other nations have trust in the United States. The release of any internationally sensitive information is not in our country's best interest at this time.

(Kim Jong Un)

SINS

OF

OUR

PRESIDENTS

All Presidents have goals of what they want to accomplish. They also have options on how to achieve those goals, which includes covert operations which are most often carried out by the CIA. All Senators have access to intelligence information including covert operations.

Covert operations allow a President to have Plausible deniability in the event the mission is uncovered. Uncovering missions can be embarrassing to the President, the country, or our allies. Uncovering can also put human assets a risk.

By law, the President is required to ensure that the Committee is kept fully and currently informed of intelligence activities—meaning that intelligence agencies are required, generally in writing, to notify the Committee of its activities and analysis. This includes keeping the Committee informed of covert actions and any significant intelligence failure.

Every President makes a mark in history. The legacy they leave behind is often dependent on certain facts being highlighted and other, more secretive fact remain obscured. The preservation of that legacy for at least four Presidents could become at risk if Hillary Clinton is brought to trial.

Hillary Clinton had unique access George H.W. Bush, Bill Clinton, George W. Bush, and Barack Obama and to a lesser degree Jimmy Carter through her service on his Legal Service Corporation Board.

The events listed below are not Presidential "secrets" which are much more confidential, but you still must dig deep into research to find these occurrences. They are "secret" only because people do not know to look for them. Although these events are shocking, Presidential secrets must be beyond our collective imaginations.

GEORGE H.W. BUSH

George H.W. Bush offered his assistance to his political rival and newly elected President, Bill Clinton. The information provided Bill Clinton was highly valued given the Bush Sr. was a President, Vice President, and most importantly former Director of the CIA. They became very close with Bush referring to Bill Clinton as being like a son. The Bushes were less fond of Hillary.

Bush likely shared information about overt and covert operations in Panama and during the first gulf war. Although most of these operations are not secret they are well hidden. Only those who search for this information of these events will find it. The mainstream media sanitized the information for public consumption while both wars were quite horrific.

The Panama invasion was not remotely what it was presented to be. Since it was a quick operation few people bother to research exactly what occurred. Manuel Noriega had been a CIA operative from his time as a Colonel until the day U.S. troops captured him. He reportedly earned 200,000 per year for his services. Noriega was the go between for the Iran-Contra operation.

(Manuel Noriega)

The 9000 U.S. troops in addition to the 12,000 U.S. troops already stationed in Panama met little resistance from the 3000 Panamanian troops. An estimated 6000 people, mostly civilians, were killed in the invasion. Many were crushed by tanks rolling over stationary cars caught in traffic. Reports of mass graves in Panama City being torched by U.S. troops using flame-throwers were reported by locals.

The official rationale for invading Panama was that we were protecting American lives, saving Panamanian people from brutality and freeing a country from a thug. None of these explanations makes much sense.

Bush claimed saving Panama's people from brutality was a goal of the invasion. The U.S. has never had qualms about brutalizing the Panamanian people; not during this invasion and not during the previous 83 years of U.S. domination. In the 1989 invasion, U.S. firepower was turned on civilian communities. The poor working-class neighborhood of El Chorillo was burnt to the ground. An estimated 6000 civilians were killed. This invasion was not done to protect Panama's people.

Bush claimed protecting American lives was a goal of the invasion. Panamanian troops killed a U.S soldier. Bush said this meant all Americans stationed in Panama were in danger. This was a false flag event. The U.S. government had been provoking such an incident for months by running military exercises through the streets of Panama City. A schoolteacher was killed by U.S. troops in one exercise. In this artificially tense climate, U.S. soldiers ran a Panamanian checkpoint near a sensitive military installation and one of them got shot. Given the U.S. troops were well equipped and outnumbered the Panamanian Military in the country by four times the number, Panama was no threat to U.S. troops. U.S. troops in Panama served the U.S. economic, military, and political domination of Panama. Protecting their safety meant tightening that domination.

Bush claimed the invasion was to free a country from a thug. General Noriega was a military officer handpicked and trained by U.S. to run Panama. He became a paid CIA operative in 1967 and attended the U.S. Army's notorious School of the Americas (also known as the School of Assassins). When the previous Panamanian leader Omar Torrijos fell out of U.S. favor (and then fell out of the sky in a 1981 plane crash), Manuel Noriega was hoisted into power with U.S. backing.

Noriega certainly was a corrupt and vicious thug. This was why Noriega was a valuable asset, as a ruthless man whose loyalty could be bought, who would do whatever was needed to serve U.S. interests, including suppress the Panamanian people.

Under Noriega, U.S. military operations expanded in Panama. Bush, Sr. personally met with Noriega in 1967, when he was head of the CIA and in 1983, when he was Vice President. In the early '80s, Noriega helped set up the CIA's drugs-for-guns trade that used cocaine trafficking to finance their secret Contra war against Nicaragua.

The U.S. government, and Bush Sr. personally, had imposed this brutal agent on Panama for many years. Elite U.S. forces seized Noriega and flew him to the U.S. to stand trial and to ensure that he was never allowed to spill all the secrets he knew about the CIA and George Bush.

Bush claimed the U.S. was restoring democracy in Panama, even though we had installed Noriega and his predecessor Torrijos. Guillermo Endara became the U.S. government's hand-picked choice and was sworn in as President of Panama, on a U.S. base, in the U.S.-controlled Canal Zone. The new Panamanian President and others in his government were tied to Panamanian banks that were deep into drug trade and money laundering. None of these leaders came to power to serve the Panamanian people. Perhaps it was a new version of democracy.

Carter had started the process of turning control of the canal over to Panama. Bush knew that without a U.S. presence, the Panama Canal would be at risk for foreign invasion and that Noriega would be powerless to stop it. Bush also knew Noriega would be able to blackmail the new President over secret CIA dealings of which they both shared knowledge and complicity.

Bush Sr.'s other main foe was Saddam Hussein of Iraq. Hussein was also a former CIA operative and rose to power with the help of the CIA.

(Saddam Hussein)

In the past, Saddam was seen by U.S. intelligence services as a bulwark of anti-communism and they used him as their instrument for more than 40 years. While many have thought that Saddam first became involved with U.S. intelligence agencies at the start of the September 1980 Iran-Iraq war, his first contacts with U.S. officials date back to 1959, when he was part of a CIA-authorized six-man squad tasked with assassinating then Iraqi Prime Minister Gen. Abd al-Karim Qasim. In July 1958, Qasim had overthrown the Iraqi monarchy.

Iraq was then regarded as a key buffer and strategic asset in the Cold War with the Soviet Union. In the mid-1950s, Iraq joined the anti-Soviet Baghdad Pact which was to defend the region and whose members included Turkey, Britain, Iran and Pakistan.

Little attention was paid to Qasim's bloody and conspiratorial regime until his sudden decision to withdraw from the pact in 1959. Qasim began to buy arms from the Soviet Union and put his own domestic communists into ministry positions of power.

Saddam, while only in his early 20s, became a part of a U.S. plot to get rid of Qasim. Saddam was installed in an apartment in Baghdad directly opposite Qasim's office to observe Qasim's movements.

(Abd al-Karim Qasim)

The move was done with full knowledge of the CIA. Saddam's CIA handler was an Iraqi dentist working for CIA and Egyptian intelligence. The assassination was set for Oct. 7, 1959, but it was completely botched. Accounts differ. One former CIA official said that the 22-

year-old Saddam lost his nerve and began firing too soon, killing Qasim's driver and only wounding Qasim in the shoulder and arm.

Saddam then crossed into Syria and was transferred by Egyptian intelligence agents to Beirut. While Saddam was in Beirut, the CIA paid for Saddam's apartment and put him through a brief training course. The agency then helped him get to Cairo. In Cairo, Saddam was installed in an apartment in the upper-class neighborhood. During this time Saddam was making frequent visits to the American Embassy where CIA specialists were in residence and knew Saddam.

In February 1963 Qasim was killed in a Baath Party coup. The CIA was suspected to be behind the coup. Noting that the Baath Party was hunting down Iraq's communists, the CIA provided the Iraqi National Guardsmen with lists of suspected communists who were then jailed, interrogated, and summarily gunned down. Many suspected communists were killed outright. Mass killings were often presided over by Saddam.

The CIA's relationship with Saddam intensified after the start of the Iran-Iraq war in September of 1980. During the war, the CIA regularly sent a team to Saddam to deliver battlefield intelligence obtained from Saudi AWACS surveillance aircraft to aid the effectiveness of Iraq's armed forces.

The Saddam-U.S. intelligence alliance of convenience ended on Aug. 2, 1990, when 100,000 Iraqi troops, backed by 300 tanks, invaded its neighbor, Kuwait. America's one-time ally had become its bitterest enemy.

*According to Ditz, Jason, 2011, the Glaspie memo
was released by WikiLeaks. The cable details the
meeting between US Ambassador April Glaspie and
Saddam Hussein just a week before the Iraqi invasion
of Kuwait.*

*It had long been speculated that comments by
Glaspie had led Saddam to believe that the United
States was giving them the green light to invade
Kuwait.*

*Glaspie assured Saddam of Bush's friendship and
expressed support for the negotiations. She also
explicitly said the United States took no position on
the border dispute between Iraq and Kuwait, though
the summary also mentions that she made clear the
US wanted the move solved peacefully. Hussein
assured that no action would be taken against Kuwait
if the negotiations showed some progress, which
seemed to suit the US at the time.*

*But the talks didn't accomplish anything and by
August 2 Iraq was invading Kuwait. A few months
later the US invaded for the first time.*

Speculation surrounded the first Iraq war because
Saddam was also in a position (like Noriega) to expose CIA
actions and operatives. The Glaspie memo had been kept
secret and while Saddam publicly touted that the
Ambassador had given tacit permission for him to invade
Kuwait, the matter remained classified, until it was brought
to light through Wikileaks. It is speculated that Bush lured
Saddam into the war, and had it not been for world-wide
condemnation of U.S. attacks on retreating Iraqi troops, a

full-on invasion of Iraq would likely have taken place, including toppling Saddam Hussein.

<u>BILL CLINTON</u>

Bill Clinton famously declared Hillary Clinton Co-President and changed her role from traditional First Lady to one of his advisors. She was privileged to secrets during this time and due to their interdependency, likely knew things even other advisors did not.

As long as they can tolerate each other and remain married, his secrets are safe. Hillary cannot be compelled to testify against her husband. They have collectively faced several scandals and are likely to face more in the future. That does not necessarily mean that some of his misdeeds would not be brought to light should Hillary be prosecuted but they both are notorious for using "I do not recall" defense.

The Democratic Republic of Congo is a very poor country, but it has enormous wealth within its interior rainforest. The rainforest region houses gold, silver, oil, and uranium. The uranium is the purest in the world and while the U.S. has uranium supplies of its own, the uranium used to create the first nuclear bombs which were dropped on Japan during World War 2 came from the Congo. It is another material that is rarer that comes from the rainforest; Coltan that makes this region coveted. 80% of all the Coltan in the world comes from the rainforest area of the Congo. Coltan is a metal used to make cell phones and video games.

The United States has had unparalleled influence over the Congo ever since Belgium released colonial rule. It has installed and removed leaders. The U.S. goals have always been to exploit the riches of the rainforest by multi-national corporations. It has done little to help the people of the Congo and has ignored the horrific genocide which has killed more than 10 million Congolese people. Events in the Congo have almost entirely ignored by the U.S. news.

According to Ray, Ellen, 2000, *The United States' involvement in Congo since before independence from Belgium in June 1960 has been steady, sinister, and penetrating. Most notable was the CIA's role in the overthrow and later assassination of Congo's first Prime Minister, the charismatic (and socialist) Patrice Lumumba. The full extent of U.S. machinations was not known for years, but the failure at the time of the United Nations to protect Lumumba was patent. And questions continue to linger over the mysterious plane crash in September 1961 that killed U.N. Secretary General Dag Hammarskjold as he was flying to meet with Moise Tshombe, President of the breakaway Katanga Province. The plane fell from*

*the sky killing all aboard. The Congo has little trust
of Washington or respect for the United Nations.*

*In October 1996, the Alliance of Democratic Forces
for the Liberation of Congo commanded by of Tutsi
military forces from Paul Kagame's Rwanda
Patriotic Army, along with Tutsi refugees and under
the leadership of Congolese Kabila, crossed into
Congo from Rwanda and Burundi. After only seven
months of fighting, they had overthrown the 30-year
dictatorship of Mobutu.*

(Mobutu Sese Seku)

*In Kinshasa, with Kabila named President, key
cabinet posts and the new Congo army and security
forces were immediately staffed at the highest levels
by Rwandan Tutsis.*

*By July 1998, Kabila realized that the Congolese
people would not support the excesses of the*

Rwandan "foreigners" throughout their government. He also recognized the extent to which he had become a puppet of his Tutsi "allies," and after confirmed reports of atrocities by Tutsi military against Hutu exiles in the east, and later in the west of the country, had become too prevalent to ignore, and after he had uncovered an apparent Rwandan plot to assassinate him and stage a coup in Congo, Kabila ordered the Rwandans to leave.

Less than a week later, on August 2, 1998, Ugandan and Rwandan regular troops invaded Congo with regrouped, well-trained rebel forces, and began the war to overthrow Kabila that goes on to this day despite a shaky, much-violated, U.S.-supported cease-fire. Rwandans and Ugandans control most of the east of the country, and there has been a de facto partition, a gross violation of Congolese sovereignty.

(Laurent Kabila)

*Rwanda is a tiny impoverished nation, and Uganda is
not much larger or richer, while Congo is one of the
largest, richest, and most populous nations in Africa,
which at one time had its most powerful army
Rwanda and Uganda could not have orchestrated,
armed, and financed such operations on their own.*

*Rwandan strongman Paul Kagame was trained in the
United States. The Rwandan army received training
in the U.S.. The Pentagon had Special Forces
military training missions in Rwanda and Uganda for
more than five years. Vast segments of the Congolese
infrastructure, particularly the mining companies,
have been taken over by U.S.- and western-linked
multinationals, working with the Rwandan and
Ugandan rebels and governments.*

*The Mobutu era began with ardent U.S. support,
financial and military. From 1965 to 1991, Congo
received more than $1.5 billion in U.S. economic and
military aid. In return, U.S. multinationals increased
their share of the ownership of Congo's fabulous
mineral wealth. Mobutu's corruption and brutality
were ignored for thirty years. It was only when the
plunder of western-owned assets and the ruination of
the country were nearly complete, when Mobutu's
stolen billions had become a worldwide
embarrassment, that the U.S. began to seek an
acceptable change.*

*America all but ignored the Rwandan massacres in
the spring of 1994 which was one reason it later
sided with the triumphant victims. The U.S. became
increasingly close to the Rwandan government and
the army that backed it. Washington pumped military*

*aid into Kagame's army and U. S. Army Special
Forces and other military personnel trained
hundreds of Rwandan forces."*

(Paul Kagame)

*The U.S. mounted a humanitarian operation in
Rwanda, but which also included training Rwandan
military in combat, counterinsurgency, psychological
operations, etc.. The role of the Rwanda and Uganda
in neighboring Congo is a classic example of U.S.
meddling.*

*The full extent of U.S. military support for Kagame's
move, against Mobutu and Congo is unclear. In
August 1996, six weeks before Kabila's forces moved
into Congo, Kagame had visited Washington.
Kagame was prepared to act, and that this was
certainly in the U.S. government's interest. In
October 1996, the full-scale incursion began, much
of eastern Congo was immediately taken.*

Kabila relied heavily on the well-trained Rwandan officers, along with Rwandan, Angolan, and Ugandan troops, to push Mobutu's army aside. The U.S. denied any ties to Kabila and denied that any foreign forces were fighting with him. Diplomatic signals, however, got crossed:

At the start of the rebellion, the U.S. Ambassador to Rwanda, denied in the face of mounting evidence that the Rwandan army had any role in the action in eastern Congo. But at the same time, in Mobutu's capital, Kinshasa, American Envoy to Congo, was denouncing the uprising as a Rwandan and Ugandan invasion. U.S. policy initially was divided. The Pentagon helped Rwanda while the State Department pretended the situation wasn't happening. It is certain that the U.S. helped overthrow Mobutu.

A South African pilot flew a planeload of assault rifles to Burundi, where he was met by an official from the U.S. Embassy. The weapons were destined for Mr. Kabila's revolt. In November, "senior officers from the U.S. Embassy in Rwanda were seen leaving Mr. Kabila's residence in Goma. By spring, a State Department official, Dennis Hankins, was ensconced in a local hotel in Goma "as the first full-time American diplomat posted to the capital of the rebel alliance. In April, the House passed a resolution calling on Mobutu to step down.

Despite U.S. approval of and involvement in the overthrow of Mobutu, U.S. support for Kabila from the beginning was mixed, and hostility later intensified.

*Kabila's new government began to clean up the
capital and restore the country's infrastructure,
bringing a semblance of normalcy to their lives.
15,000 young soldiers patrolling Kinshasa did not
speak the language and were strangers to the city
Locals refused to have anything to do with them.
Most of Kabila's government was staffed by
Rwandans as was his security and military. Rumors
that Kabila was Rwandan and not Congolese began
to circulate.*

*The demand that the massacres committed during the
overthrow of Mobutu be fully investigated and that
the perpetrators be identified and punished was
raised, but the U.N. and the Clinton administration
never revealed what they knew. Kabila responded by
claiming that countries and international groups
must assume some of the responsibility. He stopped
short of conceding that Rwandan troops, in fact,
committed mass killings in their sweep across the
country but he hinted at complicity by both the U.S.
government and certain human rights groups.*

*Clinton visited Congo in 1998. His main interest was
the protection of the U.S. multinational companies
operating in the rainforest. He asked Kabila to cede
the territory to Rwanda, a request that was rejected.
Only four months after President Clinton's trip to
Africa, Kabila ordered all Rwandan and Ugandan
Tutsi troops out of the country. On July 28, 1998,
they began to leave, taking much of what was left of
the DRC treasury with them. Kabila later described a
foiled assassination attempt against him as the factor
that precipitated the ouster.*

On August 2, only four days later, Rwanda and Uganda invaded Congo from the east with ground troops from their regular armies. And just two days after that, in what must have involved months of forward planning, there were two airborne invasions by Rwanda in the west, and Ugandan troops simultaneously landed in the south and occupied the ports. An attempted coup was under way.

Eastern Congo, virtually annexed by Uganda and Rwanda, is one of the most mineral-rich areas in the world. Gold and diamonds and rare strategic minerals are flowing into the two countries, earning vast sums for their treasures. The border between Congo and Rwanda is a mere formality. The international mining companies that operate in Kivu protect the Rwandans, who have a monopoly on the mining and marketing of those minerals.

By the end of the year, pressures on Kabila to enter talks were overpowering, even though it had become clear to the world that Congo had been invaded and occupied by foreign powers and was not in the throes of a civil war.

Kabila was assassinated in 2001. He was replaced by his son, Joseph Kabila.

The failure of both Bill Clinton and George W. Bush to express even the most perfunctory regret over the assassination of Congo President Kabila betrays how implicated Washington is in this latest outrage against the most important country in central Africa.

Washington's silence is even more glaring considering that its foreign policy experts understand the

African people view the secret intelligence agencies of the U.S. government, which work closely with corporations seeking vast fortunes in the region, as the probable authors of this crime.

American Mineral Fields (AMFI), a consortium based originally in Hope, Ark., Bill Clinton's hometown is a big player in exploiting Congo's mineral wealth.

This project is part of the $60-billion National Missile Defense system that the Bush, administration pushed vigorously. Building the space station will require many of the rare metals found in eastern Congo.

Another big player in the eastern Congo is Barrick Gold Corp., headquartered in Canada. It is the world's second-largest gold producer after Anglo-American of South Africa. George Bush Sr. sat on the board of directors of Barrick.

<u>GEORGE W. BUSH</u>

The Presidency of George W. Bush was ripe with unprecedented events. The attack on the World Trade

Center and Pentagon remains fresh in many of our minds today. The original plan called for 10 airplanes and the planned attacks included the Bank of America Tower in Seattle, Alameda Naval Base, Sears Tower, Disney World, Disney Land, an unspecified movie studio and the plane that crashed over Pennsylvania was heading for the U.S. Capital Building.

The plane that passengers deliberately crashed in Pennsylvania is a favorite topic of conspiracy theorists. Part of the reason is that George W. Bush did indeed give the order for it to be shot down. The only planes able to reach it in time were unarmed planes flown by the National Guard. Two brave pilots were prepared to fly their jets into the airliner to bring it down, but when they arrived, the plane had already crashed.

The 9-11 attacks started a war in Afghanistan and Iraq. The wars preoccupied much of the terms of the President. The attacks caused Americans to sacrifice freedoms for security through the Patriot Act. The events brought about discussions about how to treat enemy combatants many of which underwent torture in Guantanamo Bay. During the first four years, the President was kept in the dark about the extent of torture used as well as its ineffectiveness. The CIA was more worried about the reaction of Colin Powell to the news than they were about the President's reaction.

Just one month prior to the 911 attack, the Taliban had reneged on a deal to allow construction of an oil pipeline from Kazakhstan through Afghanistan. At the same time, Qatar was pushing to build a pipeline through Iraq. Both of these projects would require continuation through Syria, which of course is currently at war. While the wars in the middle east distracted most of us, there were more secret actions occurring in South America.

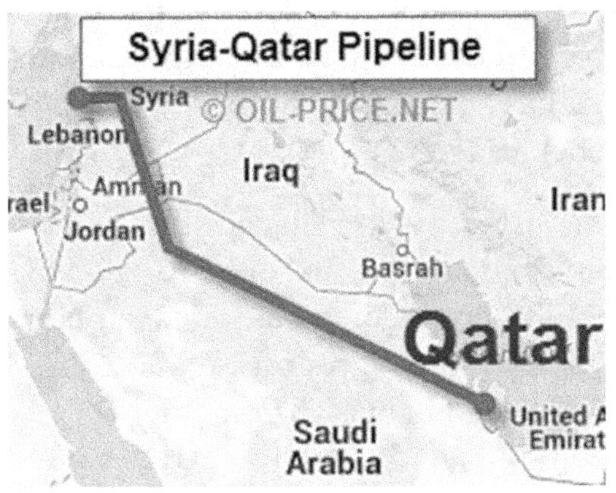

(Planned Qatari Pipeline)

A recent report has exposed a secret CIA program in Colombia that has helped kill at least two dozen rebel leaders. The program relies on key help from the National Security Agency and is funded through a multibillion-dollar black budget. It began under former President George W. Bush. The program has crippled the FARC rebel group by targeting its leaders using bombs equipped with GPS guidance. The CIA controlled the encryption keys that allowed the bombs to read GPS data. In one case, in 2008, the United States and Colombia discovered a FARC leader hiding in Ecuador. According to the report, to conduct an airstrike meant a Colombian pilot flying a Colombian plane would hit the camp using a U.S.-made bomb with a CIA-controlled brain. The attack killed the rebel leader and sparked a major flareup of tensions with Ecuador and Venezuela. The U.S. role in that attack had not previously been reported.

The 50-year-old Revolutionary Armed Forces of Colombia (FARC), once considered the best-funded insurgency in the world, is at its smallest and most vulnerable state in decades, due in part to a CIA covert action program that has helped Colombian forces kill at least two dozen rebel leaders.

The secret assistance also included substantial eavesdropping help from the National Security Agency, funded through a multibillion-dollar black budget. It was not a part of the public $9 billion package of mostly U.S. military aid called Plan Colombia. The program is classified and ongoing.

The covert program in Colombia provides two essential services to Colombia. Real-time intelligence that allows Colombian forces to hunt down individual FARC leaders and an effective tool with which to kill them. That weapon is a $30,000 GPS guidance kit that transforms a less-than-accurate 500-pound gravity bomb into a highly accurate smart bomb. Smart bombs are capable of killing an individual in dense jungle if his exact location can be determined and geo-coordinates are programmed into the bomb's small computer brain.

The covert action program in Colombia is one of a handful of enhanced intelligence initiatives that has escaped public notice since the Sept. 11, 2001, attacks. Most of these other programs, small but growing, are in countries where violent drug cartels have caused instability.

As a Senator at the time, Hillary Clinton would have had access to intelligence materials regarding these and other covert operations.

BARRACK OBAMA

Despite an ugly primary, Obama welcomed Clinton into his fold and chose her to be Secretary of State. Not only was she in a position to know his secret operations but to be complicit with them while creating some of her own.

President Obama's fast and the furious scandal is well known now. Obama authorized high grade weapons delivered to cartels in Mexico as a way to track the cartels. Once those weapons were used to kill border guards the secrecy of the operation unraveled.

Obama conducted extensive domestic surveillance in the name of fighting terrorism despite most people being monitored having no terrorist connections. His spying extended to political opponents and members of the media. He used the IRS to harass political groups that were averse to him.

What most people do not realize is that he actually created a global army to conduct covert war in over 100 countries that, unlike the CIA, could bypass congressional oversight. Basically, he had a private army answerable only to himself.

According to Marshall, Andrew, 2013, *Obama's global terror campaign is not only dependent upon his drone assassination program, but increasingly it has come to rely upon the deployment of Special Operations forces in countries all over the world, reportedly between 70 and 120 countries at any one time. As Obama has sought to draw down the large-scale ground invasions of countries he has escalated the world of covert warfare, largely outside the oversight of Congress and the public. One of the most important agencies in this global "secret war" is the Joint Special Operations Command, or JSOC for short.*

JSOC appears to be playing an increasingly prominent role in national security and counterterrorism, in areas which were traditionally covered by the CIA. One of the most important differences between these covert warfare operations being conducted by JSOC instead of the CIA is that the CIA has to report to Congress, whereas JSOC only reports its most important activities to the President's National Security Council.

JSOC has also been involved in running a "secret war" inside of Pakistan, beginning in 2006 but accelerating rapidly under the Obama administration. The "secret war" was waged in cooperation with the CIA and the infamous private military contractor, Blackwater, made infamous for its massacre of Iraqi civilians, after which it was banned from operating in the country.

Blackwater, which primarily hires former Special Forces soldiers, has largely functioned as an overseas Praetorian guard for the CIA and State Department officials, who were also helping to craft, fund, and execute operations, including assembling hit teams, all outside of any Congressional or public oversight, since it was technically a private corporation.

The CIA hired Blackwater to aid in a secret assassination program which was hidden from Congress for seven years. These operations would be overseen by the CIA or Special Forces personnel. Blackwater has also been contracted to arm drones at secret bases in Afghanistan and Pakistan for Obama's assassination program, overseen by the CIA. The lines dividing the military, the CIA and Blackwater had become blurred.

Within the first five months of Obama's presidency in 2009, he authorized a massive expansion of clandestine military and intelligence operations worldwide, granting the Pentagon's regional combatant commanders significant new authority over such covert operations. The directive authorized Special Forces soldiers to be sent into both friendly and hostile nations in the Middle East, Central Asia and the Horn of Africa. The deployment of highly trained killers into dozens of countries was to become systemic and long term, designed to penetrate, disrupt, defeat or destroy enemies of the State, beyond the rule of law, no trial or pretenses of accountability.

They also prepare the environment for larger attacks that the U.S. or NATO countries may have planned. Unlike with the CIA, these operations do not report to Congress, or even need the President's approval. But for the big operations, they get the approval of the National Security Council, which includes the president, as well as most other major cabinet heads, of the Pentagon, CIA, State Department, etc.

Not only are U.S. forces conducting secret wars within dozens of countries around the world, but they are training the domestic military forces of many of these countries to undertake secret wars internally, and in the interests of the United States empire.

One military official even set up a network of private military corporations that hired former Special Forces and CIA operations to gather intelligence and conduct secret operations in foreign countries to support lethal action: publicly subsidized, privatized accountability. Such a network was generally considered illegal and was improperly financed. When the news of these networks emerged, the Pentagon said it shut them down and opened a criminal investigation.

Turns out, they found nothing criminal, because two months later, the operations were continuing and had become an important source of intelligence. The networks of covert-ops corporations were being managed by Lockheed Martin, one of the largest military contractors in the world, while being supervised by the Pentagon's Special Operations Command.

In 2012, it was reported that such forces would be operating in 120 different countries by the end of the year.

In short, Obama's global war of terror has expanded, increasing the small-scale warfare operations of Special Forces, beyond the rule of law, outside Congressional and public oversight, conducting snatch and grab operations, training domestic repressive military forces in nations largely run by dictatorships.

This is global warfare. Imagine for a moment the international outcry that would result from news of China or Russia conducting secret warfare operations in roughly 100 countries around the world. But when America does it, there's barely a mention.

America has long been the Global Godfather applying the 'Mafia Principles' of international relations, lock-in-step with Great Britain and France. Yet, under Obama, the president who had won public relations industry awards for his well-managed presidential advertising campaign promising "hope" and "change," the empire has found itself waging war in roughly one hundred nations, conducting an unprecedented global terror campaign, increasing its abuses of human rights, war crimes and crimes against humanity, all under the aegis of the Nobel Peace Prize-winner Barack Obama.

THE IMPACT ON NOT LOCKING HER UP

Presidents are all guaranteed a place in history books. All Presidents, but especially two term Presidents work to create a legacy that will ensure they are remembered in a good light. They do what they can to protect that legacy.

Investigating Hillary Clinton runs the risk that sensitive secrets will come to surface. The risk is greatest with her knowledge of the Obama administration since the two are complicit in several nefarious operations. Obama would likely act to protect himself, if not Hillary Clinton.

Former Presidents still hold power and influence. There are Senators and members of congress with whom they remain close. They are often called upon to endorse candidates and participate in national conventions. Those with a close connection may work to thwart any efforts that will damage the former Presidents legacy.

Former Presidents have assigned judges to lifetime positions. These judges may or may not be corrupted but the mere fact they had been appointed means they share the same constitutional interpretation as the President who assigned them to their position.

Some departmental employees always remain from the previous administration. This is to keep continuity during the transition periods. These employees are usually middle level or lower, so they may not be easy to identify. These people have the ability to lose, alter, redact, deny access to, selectively choose, delay production of or destroy evidence. Their actions may be obvious or well hidden. If called to testify they may offer little of significance, may use semantics and doubletalk, deny knowledge of evidence, or simply claim the fifth and not testify.

Losing a document is as easy as taking its contents from an identifiable file and placing them in a farm report from 1952. This is less serious than destroying the evidence, because technically the files are still intact, although locating them becomes very difficult.

Altering a document means some or all of the original material may remain, but the content has been augmented by the employee in a manner that the context may be completely changed.

Redaction is a common way to hide wrongdoing. It means the blackening out of sections or sometimes entire documents. In theory the material that is blackout is for the protection of national security but there is no way of knowing what the actual contents are.

Denying access to material is strategy often used for the highest echelon of top secret information. It can also be disguised as claiming the material is not relevant to the subpoena presented. Subpoena's for discovery information must be very specific in what is being requested. It is difficult to request documents that are not known to exist. If a document is requested and an e-mail or video of the specified event is available, it would not be voluntarily released or even acknowledged to exist if the discovery request does not specify e-mail and video. If a discovery request only asks for material created by Hillary Clinton, any ancillary staff files would not be voluntarily searched for relevance and submitted. Additional evidence may exist, but it will not be volunteered.

Selectively choosing what is released or the timing of the release is a way to appear that the department is being cooperative without actually being cooperative. Hillary's e-mails were released to the public slowly. The initial e-mails were innocuous. There was very little to hold the public's attention. It was not until the end of her e-mail releases that questionable material appeared. This was a way to make it appear that no damning evidence existed by selectively holding on to the damning material for later release, once the public's interest had waned. The FBI made attempts to delay the release of more sensitive material until after the election.

Destruction of evidence is the most serious offense. If a cell phone is requested into evidence and the memory chip is removed and the device is smashed with a hammer, technically you would be following a court order but not the spirit of the law. The same would be the case if you remove the hard drive from a computer or smash the computer prior to turning it over to evidence. Shredding material in governmental agencies is common practice as well. Anticipating what may be requested and damning may result in preemptive destruction of documents prior to a subpoena.

Any case against Hillary Clinton is going to be highly dependent on a factual document trail that cannot be impeached. Such a trail, if it exists, will be very difficult to obtain and its integrity will be questioned by the opposition team.

If evidence is not enough to prosecute, then witnesses are called. The Clinton's themselves are masters at semantics and double talk. They always leave enough wiggle room so that if they are caught in a lie, they can declare what they said was taken out of context. It's called Clintonese. This approach makes them look as though they are being cooperative when they are not. Others use this technique as well.

Denying direct knowledge of an event or pleading the 5th is another tactic used by potential witnesses to avoid answering questions in court. Loretta Lynch used this technique. Brian Pagliano, Clinton's IT manager, who set up her server, invoked the 5th amendment 125 times during his testimony.

By protecting the legacy of a President, these embedded people can make prosecution impossible, even if they choose to remain, technically, within the law.

THE
INTEGRITY
OF
THE
GOVERNMENT

In order for people to have confidence in their government they must trust the institutions of that government. Under the Obama administration the trust in many governmental departments has eroded. It is important to rebuild trust in these departments if people are to remain confident in the government's ability to govern. It is essential to rebuild that trust if Hillary Clinton is to be prosecuted.

The Internal Revenue Service (IRS)

According to Boehm, Ken, 2013, *America can handle the truth. Even if that truth could include a coverup at the powerful IRS. The IRS mission statement pledges to enforce the law with integrity and fairness to all. But public scrutiny has revealed details indicating a level of politicization totally at odds with that.*

Look at the two eye-opening developments that have happened at the IRS; an acting IRS commissioner resigned, and another powerful IRS official refused to answer questions before Congress, pleading the Fifth Amendment.

The IRS inspector general released a report describing how the agency had inappropriately targeted tea party and conservative groups that had applied for tax-exempt status. The IRS put these groups through extra reviews, substantial delays and burdensome requests for information. The reaction was immediate. The next day, President Barack Obama announced that the acting IRS commissioner was resigning. Obama went on to say, "I will not tolerate this kind of behavior in any agency, but especially in the IRS, given the power that it has and the reach that it has into all of our lives." After that shocking disclosure, several things happened; Senate and House committees launched investigations into the scandal, the FBI began a criminal investigation, the IRS inspector general expanded its ongoing investigation, and IRS official Lois Lerner exercised her Fifth Amendment right against self-incrimination by refusing to answer questions before Congress.

(Lois Lerner)

Some interesting developments emerged from all that. The original claim during IRS testimony that the scandal was the result of a couple of rogue IRS agents in the agency's Cincinnati field office didn't hold water. It turned out that the Washington IRS office had played a key role in the handling of the tea party applications.

Montana Democrat Sen. Max Baucus, the committee chairman, stated bluntly, "Targeting groups based on their political views is not only inappropriate, it is intolerable, unacceptable and cannot be allowed."

The chairman of the ethics watchdog group National Legal and Policy Center, filed a complaint with the IRS showing that a purported charity called the Barack H. Obama Foundation, named for the father of President Obama and run by his half-brother, Malik Obama had been raising funds in the U.S. by falsely claiming to be an IRS-approved charitable group.

There was compelling evidence suggesting that the foundation was raising money on the Internet by misrepresenting itself as being IRS-approved when it really wasn't. Suddenly, the foundation rushed an application to the IRS. In the short span of about a month, Lerner, the same person who took the Fifth Amendment rather than testify before Congress gave the Obama Foundation its tax-deductible status. And, the IRS made that status retroactive for three years. Even more curious, several of the forms submitted by Malik Obama were stamped as being received by the IRS in July 2011. That's one month after Lerner approved the group's new tax status.

The final results, as oft touted by liberals, is that there is no evidence that conservative groups were targeted. They point to the fact that some liberal groups were also given added scrutiny. Of the 450 plus groups targeted, there were a couple that were liberal minded. This does not justify Malik Obama's foundation receiving quick approval that was retroactive, Lois Lerner pleading the fifth, and the destruction of her computer and records. Regardless of the results of this investigation, confidence in the IRS has been shaken. The damage is done and must be repaired in order to restore public trust.

<u>The National Security Agency (NSA)</u>

According to Westby, Jody, 2014, *It has been revealed that the NSA is capturing information by exploiting mobile phones and gaming, social media, and mapping applications. The NSA can obtain a treasure trove of information from a smart phone, including location, phone settings, websites visited, networks connected, documents downloaded, and buddy lists.*

Prior to June 5, 2013, Americans generally believed their government was working hard to detect and prevent terrorist activities and attacks within the U.S. They also generally believed that whatever spying the U.S. intelligence community was up to was targeted at foreigners, not the American public. They now know that those general assumptions were not accurate. Through the many disclosures made since then, the people of the U.S. now know that.

The NSA has been collecting data about every telephone call they have made, the number that was called, and the duration of the call. (Snowden revealed the Verizon court order, and it is now widely believed that other providers have received similar orders).

According to NSA PRISM program documents, the NSA has been collecting every form of electronic communication conceivable directly from Microsoft, Yahoo!, PalTalk, Google, Facebook, YouTube, Skype, AOL, and Apple.The documents indicate it includes the content of Internet phone calls, chat, photos, emails, stored data, video conferencing, and text messages.

(Edward Snowden)

The NSA has been intercepting communications at the backbone of major communications providers.

The companies that have been ordered to participate in NSA surveillance programs by a Foreign Intelligence Surveillance Court order are forbidden by law from disclosing any information about the order. Many of the technology companies have tried to pressure the Obama Administration to let them provide information to the public about their participation. The NSA can keep and use communications on U.S. residents without a warrant for five years.

Intelligence officials have not been truthful about their surveillance programs.The Director of National Intelligence, James Clapper, lied to Congress about what communications it was collecting on Americans when he answered Sen. Ron Wyden's question, "Does the NSA collect any type of data at all on millions or hundreds of millions of Americans?" Mr. Clapper answered, "No sir."

The leaked intelligence budget revealed that the NSA is spending billions of taxpayer dollars on these programs. Many members of Congress were not aware of the full extent of the programs and their reach into American's daily lives and communications.

The necessity of the data for national security purposes is questionable. No terrorist attack has been stopped due to data collected by the program.

Snowden has not been careful to release only information that impacted Americans' civil liberties. Within the first ten days of his disclosure campaign, Snowden had provided documents indicating that the NSA was spying on computers in China and Hong Kong, hacking into Chinese backbone providers to steal mobile text messages, and attacking the network of one of China's top universities, Tsinghua University. He then revealed information about NSA's spying on Angela Merkel and other allied leaders and collaborative intelligence sharing programs between the U.S. and the "Five Eyes" (U.S., U.K., Canada, Australia, and New Zealand).

Since this publication, it has been discovered that the Members of the House and Senate, Members of the American Media and Members of the Trump campaign have also fallen victim to the extensive surveillance powers assumed by the NSA.

There has been some good that has come from the surveillance operations in combatting drug trade and the distribution of child pornography but that is not the purpose of the Patriot Act and Freedom Act's mission. The NSA has also gone far beyond the scope of who and what they can monitor and for what purpose. The information they gather is shared amongst many governmental departments.

The Department of Interior

President Obama federalized more land than any other President; 553 million acres. He designated the land as National monuments which can be done without congressional approval, unlike National Parks. He has been lauded by native tribes and environmental groups for his protection of the environment.

The truth is very different though. It is a land grab. Mining, drilling, forestry and cattle driving can still occur on this land, it is now regulated by the federal government and not the state or private owners. Oddly much of the land designated by Obama is rich in uranium deposits. The Interior Department played a vital role in the controversial Uranium One sale.

The Interior Department is a money-making department. While the state loses incomes through taxing operations on the land and those who work in those operations, the federal government makes large amounts of money by selling the rights to procure, minerals, gas and oil. The Department became embroiled in a wide-ranging scandal under the Bush and Obama administrations.

According to Savage, Charlie, 2008, *as Congress prepares to debate expansion of drilling in taxpayer-owned coastal waters, the Interior Department agency that collects oil and gas royalties has been caught up in a wide-ranging ethics scandal, including allegations of financial self-dealing, accepting gifts from energy companies, cocaine use and sexual misconduct.*

In three reports delivered to Congress on Wednesday, the department's inspector general, Earl E. Devaney, found wrongdoing by a dozen current and former employees of the Minerals Management Service, which collects about $10 billion in royalties annually and is one of the government's largest sources of revenue other than taxes. The reports portray a dysfunctional organization that has been riddled with conflicts of interest, unprofessional behavior, and a free-for-all.

While previous reports have focused on problems the agency had in collecting millions of dollars owed to the Treasury, and hinted at personal misconduct, the new reports go far beyond any previous study in revealing serious concerns with the integrity and behavior of the agency's officials.

In one of the new reports, investigators concluded that Ms. Denett worked with two aides to steer a lucrative consulting contract to one of the aides after he retired, violating competitive procurement rules. Two other reports focus on a culture of substance *abuse and promiscuity in the service's royalty-in-kind program. That part of the agency collects about $4 billion a year in oil and gas rather than cash royalties.*

Based in suburban Denver and modeled to operate like a private sector energy company, the decade-old royalty-in-kind program sells oil and gas on the open market. Its employees are subject to government ethics rules, such as restrictions on taking gifts from people and companies with whom they conduct official business.

One of the reports says that the officials viewed themselves as exempt from those limits, indulging themselves in the expense-account-fueled world of oil and gas executives.

The report says that eight officials in the royalty program accepted gifts from energy companies whose value exceeded limits set by ethics rules including golf, ski and paintball outings; meals and drinks; and tickets to a Toby Keith concert, a Houston Texans football game and a Colorado Rockies baseball game.

The investigation also concluded that several of the officials frequently consumed alcohol at industry functions, had used cocaine and marijuana, and had sexual relationships with oil and gas company representatives. The culture of the organization appeared to be devoid of both the ethical standards and internal controls sufficient to protect the integrity of this vital revenue-producing program.

The inspector general urged the administration to take action against several of the officials in the royalty-in-kind program who accepted gifts from the oil companies, by firing them or banning them for life from certain positions. Several have already been transferred out of the program but remain on the government payroll.

But two of the highest-ranking officials who were subjects of the investigations will apparently escape penalty. Both retired during the investigation, rendering them safe from any administrative punishment, and the Justice Department has declined to prosecute them on the charges suggested by the inspector general.

One of them is Ms. Denett, who oversaw the Denver-based royalty-in-kind program from Washington. The report contends that she manipulated the contracting process to steer the consulting work to Mr. Mayberry, her friend and former special assistant.

Six other companies submitted bids for the contract, spending more than $90,000 on their proposals. The report said an Interior Department procurement lawyer described the arrangement as one in which "the fix is in throughout this is tainted from the beginning, that is totally improper.

The report also said that Mr. Smith improperly used his position with the royalty program to get an outside consulting job helping a technical services firm seek deals with oil and gas companies with which he was also conducting official business.

The report accused Mr. Smith of improperly accepting gifts from the oil and gas industry, of engaging in sex with two subordinates and of using cocaine that he purchased from his secretary or her boyfriend. He sometimes asked for the drugs and received them in his office during work hours. The report also said that Mr. Smith lied to investigators about these and other incidents, and that he urged the two women subordinates to mislead the investigators as well.

The report also detailed cozy relationships between energy companies and other officials in the royalty-in-kind program office. Some 19 officials, a third of the staff, took gifts from oil and gas executives, some with great frequency.

On one occasion two of the officials who marketed taxpayers' oil got so drunk at a daytime golfing event sponsored by Shell that they could not drive to their hotels and were put up in Shell-provided lodging. On another occasion, one of the officials shared information about the confidential price a pipeline company was charging the government. The officials told investigators that the gifts and socializing did not affect how they treated the companies in their official duties.

<u>The Attorney General's Office (AG) under Holder</u>

According to Wyler, Grace, 2012, *President Barack Obama asserted executive privilege over documents related to the Operation Fast and Furious, setting off a Washington firestorm over his administration's botched gun-running operation.*

The move comes on the same day that House Oversight had scheduled a contempt vote against Obama's Attorney General Eric Holder over his refusal to turn over documents related to the Operation Fast and Furious, in which U.S. agents allowed guns to "walk" across the border into Mexico.

(Eric Holder)

Obama's use of executive privilege, the first such action of his presidency upped the political profile of the gun-running scandal.

Operation Fast and Furious was launched in 2009 by top DOJ officials, in collaboration with the FBI, the Drug Enforcement Agency, and the Bureau of Alcohol, Tobacco, and Firearms (ATF) as part of a strategy to identify and eliminate arms trafficking networks. Instead of prosecuting the individual who buy guns for the cartels, ATF agents would track the guns to the top bosses of Mexico's powerful drug cartels.

Fast and Furious was the biggest gun-walking operation that the DOJ had ever undertaken. ATF agents allowed more than 2,000 firearms to "walk" across the border. As many as 1,700 of those weapons have since been lost, and more than 100 have been found at bloody crime scenes on both sides of the border, including the murder of a U.S. Border Patrol agent in Arizona last December.

ATF whistle-blowers blew the lid from Operation Fast and Furious shortly after the Border Patrol Agent's death. The Justice Department denied the existence of Operation Fast and Furious, writing that the ATF makes every effort to interdict weapons that have been purchased illegally and prevent their transportation to Mexico. Evidence later emerged revealing that senior Justice Department officials knew about Operation Fast and Furious months before the letter was sent. The DOJ acknowledged that the letter was inaccurate, and turned over about 1,400 pages of documents to prove to Congress that it didn't deliberately try to mislead Congress.

Holder came under fire from Congress, after he told the Oversight Committee in May 2011 that he first

*heard of Fast and Furious "over the last few weeks."
But Congress later obtained internal DOJ memos
related to the Operation that were addressed to
Holder and dated from Sept. 2010.*

*Obama's executive privilege now protects those post-
Feb. 4 documents from Congressional subpoena,
meaning that the DOJ won't have to provide the
documents. In his request for executive privilege,
Holder argued that the documents should be
protected from subpoena because they were not
related to Operation Fast and Furious, but rather to
how DOJ was going to respond to congressional and
media inquiries about the operation.*

*As far as we can tell, the legal premise of Holder's
argument is sound, allowing the House to control
how the executive branch responds to investigations
would be a violation of the balance of powers. Plus,
there's precedent, previous presidents, including
George W. Bush and Bill Clinton, used executive
privilege for the same reasons that Holder lays out.*

*Obama's decision to further enshroud the Fast and
Furious scandal in secrecy confirms suspicions that
the administration is hiding something, and is
possibly trying to cover up who knew what about the
botched gun-walking program.*

<u>The Attorney General's Office (AG) under Lynch</u>

According to McCarthy, Andrew, 2016, *when it
comes to Hillary Clinton's e-mail scandal, the most
important thing to bear in mind, even more than
classified information, is that it was all about
avoiding accountability. Mrs. Clinton did not set out*

to damage national security and compromise defense secrets, although she obviously had no compunction about doing so as necessary to serve her higher personal interests.

For a generation, she has been a public person whose most intimate companion has been scandal. She knew her State Department stewardship would be no different. Her motive in designing a communication system that circumvented government recordkeeping and disclosure laws was to avoid a day of reckoning as she campaigned in 2016 for the power of the presidency she craved.

(Loretta Lynch)

Loretta Lynch came to prominence in 1999 by being appointed United States Attorney for the Eastern District of New York by none other than Mrs. Clinton's husband. Loretta Lynch, who had a history of significant political contributions to Democratic-party candidates before President Obama elevated her to U.S. Attorney General in 2015. Loretta Lynch, would have been well positioned to continue in that powerful post in a Hillary Clinton administration, had it happened.

The known evidence that Mrs. Clinton committed federal crimes is abundant, perhaps even overwhelming. It is manifest that she lawlessly transmitted and stored classified information outside its secure system, and that she allowed her underlings to do so as well. There is also the evidence that is unknown to the public though it was poured over by the FBI: the 32,000 e-mails Clinton refused to turn over to the State Department which involved converting them to her private use and attempted to destroy by trying to wipe her private server clean.

The federal embezzlement statute makes it a felony to destroy government files or convert them to one's private use. The FBI has reportedly been able to recover at least some and possibly all of the e-mails Clinton tried to erase. Unless you really believe that one of the busiest high officials in the U.S. government had time for 32,000 e-mails about yoga routines and Chelsea's wedding dress, it is inevitable that some of those e-mails related to State Department business meaning they were government files.

The Clinton e-mail scheme has always been about avoiding accountability, about denying the public a window into Hillary Clinton's disastrous decision-making, her deceptive public pronouncements, and the promiscuous interplay between State Department and Clinton Foundation business. The goal was to

Attorney General Loretta Lynch is facing a federal lawsuit to give details of a meeting she had with Bill Clinton days before she was to decide on his wife's fate. The meeting itself was improper and the secrecy behind the meeting is concerning.

They met barely a week before the Justice Department which she headed dropped its probe into Hillary Clinton's private email server.

The American Center for Law and Justice filed the lawsuit against the Department of Justice in Washington demanding more information about the meeting.

As head of the Department of Justice, Lynch was supposed to be deciding whether to proceed with charging Hillary Clinton over her unauthorized server arrangements while she was secretary of state.

Lynch's secret email address and alias were discovered by watchdog groups who were seeking answers regarding the infamous meeting between Lynch and former President Bill Clinton on a tarmac in Arizona. Loretta Lynch, via her secret e-mail, instructed James Comey to discredit the seriousness of the Clinton investigation. He was to refer to it as a matter and not an investigation.

The denial that she had a separate e-mail account directly contradicts testimony that was given under oath to Congress where she stated that she did not use any email aside from her official Justice Department email, an action that brings up the potential criminal charge of perjury.

Holder and Lynch damaged the credibility of the Justice Department. This makes the public skeptical when they don't see Attorney General Sessions rushing to a prosecution. The priority is rebuilding credibility within his department and weeding out any rogue personnel left from former administrations.

The Federal Bureau of Investigation (FBI)

When FBI Director James Comey dismissed the case against Hillary Clinton he said it was because no reasonable attorney would take the case. Now we learn that there were plenty who would have done so. When Comey made his statement about the case in July, he painted a devastating portrait of Hillary Clinton's reckless use of a private email server while Secretary of State.

(James Comey)

Clinton knew little to nothing about handling classified material. She sent and received top secret information on an unsecured private email system and was otherwise extremely careless with national security secrets. She likely exposed sensitive material to enemies, and hid thousands of work emails that were supposed to have been turned over. She or her top staff probably broke the law.

Then, Comey said that no reasonable prosecutor would bring such a case. The implication was that, while a partisan hack might bring such a case, no legitimate prosecutor would. This was an utterly false claim. Many attorneys following the case believed the Democratic presidential nominee should have been charged.

The FBI granted unusual immunity deals to key witnesses, which yielded the FBI got little or nothing of value. One of his immunity deals, for example, included an agreement that the FBI wouldn't review any emails between Cheryl Mills and Paul Combetta, the computer technician at Platte River Networks who wiped Hillary Clinton's private email server clean with BleachBit.

According to documents released by the Senate Judiciary Committee, James Comey made the decision not to refer Hillary Clinton for prosecution long before ever interviewing key witnesses. Members of the Committee allege Comey made the decision months before FBI agents were finished with the criminal investigation.

The outcome of an investigation should not be prejudged while FBI agents are still gathering facts. Conclusion first, fact-gathering second is no way to run an investigation. The FBI should be held to a higher standard than that, especially in a matter of such great public interest and controversy.

The discovery of his draft exoneration suggests former FBI Director James Comey may have committed perjury if he lied about how he came to the decision not to recommend criminal charges in the Hillary Clinton email case.

The Department of Housing (HUD)

According to Rosiak, Luke, 2016, *A federal agency will be breaking the law unless two of its top Obama administration appointees repay part of their salaries to taxpayers after barring another federal employee from telling Congress how higher-ups were allowing multi-million dollar frauds as part of a political deal.*

The Government Accountability Office (GAO) determined that the two Department of Housing and Urban Development (HUD) political appointees refused to let an employee speak with the House Committee on Oversight and Government Reform about a major scandal.

No part of any appropriation contained in this or any other act shall be available for the payment of the salary of any officer or employee of the federal government, who prohibits or prevents, or attempts or threatens to prohibit or prevent, any other officer or employee of the federal government from having any direct oral or written communication or contact with any Member, committee, or subcommittee of the Congress.

The GAO said that unless HUD's associate general counsel and a deputy assistant secretary personally return three weeks' worth of compensation, the department would be knowingly retaining improper payments on its books in violation of the law.

(Tom Perez)

The oversight panel uncovered the fact that then-Assistant Attorney General Tom Perez made a secret deal to make a potentially damaging lawsuit go away. He reportedly told the litigant that in exchange for dropping the suit, the government would look the other way on fraud the litigant was doing in an unrelated matter, which was being investigated by HUD. (Perez is now the Chairman for the DNC)

The regional director then said he had wanted to talk with Congress, but HUD's legal office told him to stop responding to the committee.

HUD's general counsel and deputy assistant secretary claimed it was not normal for Congress to interview high-ranking career bureaucrats who manage day-to-day operations and have institutional knowledge. Congress should instead talk only to political appointees who typically serve short stints in federal agencies.

They seemed to believe HUD should decide which congressional investigations into major misconduct were legitimate and which to ignore.

GAO noted that federal employees are often the source of information about agency operations suppressed by their superiors since they are much closer to the actual working situation than top agency officials.

Since HUD refused to let Congress speak with the official for six months, the salary amounts involved could have been substantial. The department claimed for those months that it was too busy with more important matters than deal with Congress. Sometimes, HUD officials didn't even reply to congressional inquiries at all.

Their delays and denials could be construed in "good faith," whereas for a three-week period they were outright refusing in bad faith. The GAO said the communications demonstrate that the delay became a denial to make the Regional Director available for interview. The GAO opinion that endless vague reasons for delay are tantamount to refusal is a warning to numerous agencies that increasingly use this approach with Congress.

<u>The Department of Education</u>

According to Bolger, Nick, 2017, *A senior Education Department official who abruptly resigned recently received hundreds of thousands of dollars in off-the-books bonuses over a seven-year period, according to a new report.*

James Runcie, an Obama administration appointee who served as chief operating officer of the Federal Student Aid office, received secret, five-figure bonuses each year while his office gave out billions in improper payments.

(James Runcie)

While Runcie ran the FSA, the government's $1.4 trillion financial aid program, the office made improper payments for the federal Pell Grant program, which ballooned from $562 million in 2015 to $2.21 billion in 2016, and for the Federal Direct

Loan program, which increased from $1.28 billion in 2015 to $3.86 billion in 2016.

These are disbursements that either shouldn't have been made, went to the wrong recipient, were for an incorrect amount, or were not properly documented. Under Runcie's leadership there was pervasive fraud and corruption at the FSA.

Runcie's personnel file showed a total of $432,885 in bonuses over a seven-year period, culminating in a $76,000 bonus in 2016. The bonuses do not appear on Runcie's official government salaries.

Runcie resigned last month after being asked to testify before Congress on the rising rate of improper payments in student aid.

<u>The State Department</u>

As Secretary of State, Clinton had a duty to protect Americans abroad. She was brought before this congressional committee to ascertain if she was negligent in fulfilling this role as it pertained to Benghazi.

After several hours of questioning Clinton lost her composure and went on the attack. Her body language, voice, facial expressions, and tone all changed. Anyone who was watching the hearings noticed. The words she spoke became a rallying cry for continued transparency on the Benghazi attack and haunted her through the 2016 election and beyond.

According to Fishel, Justin, 2015, *With all due respect, the fact is, we had four dead Americans, was it because of a protest or was it because of guys out for a walk one night and decided they'd go kill some*

Americans, what difference, at this point, does it make?!"

Americans were dead, and their deaths may have been prevented if she had not been negligent of duties.

(Hillary Clinton at Benghazi Hearings)

On September 11, 2012, the US consulate and CIA annex were attacked in Benghazi Libya. The attack resulted in the deaths of Ambassador Stevens, Information Officer Sean Smith, and two CIA operatives, Glen Doherty and Tyrone Woods. A terrorist act is often sudden and without warning. In this case, there were more than enough warning signs that the situation in Benghazi was not stable.

In April 2012, two former security guards for the consulate threw an IED over the consulate fence; the incident did not cause any casualties. Just four days later, a similar bomb was thrown at a four-vehicle convoy carrying the United Nations Special Envoy to Libya, exploding close the UN envoy's vehicle without injuring anyone. In May 2012, the International Red Cross office in Benghazi was attacked. Al-Qaeda claimed responsibility for the Red Cross attack. The Red Cross suspended operations stating they were extremely concerned about the escalating violence in Libya.

The same Al-Qaeda linked group released a video of what it said was its detonation of an explosive device outside the gates of the U.S. consulate on June 6, which caused no casualties but blew a hole in the consulate's perimeter wall. The group left behind leaflets promising more attacks against the U.S.

British ambassador to Libya Dominic Asquith survived an assassination attempt in Benghazi on June 10. Two British protection officers were injured in the attack when a rocket-propelled grenade hit their convoy. The British withdrew all consular staff from Benghazi in late June

On June 18, 2012, the Tunisian consulate in Benghazi was attacked by individuals affiliated with Ansar al-Sharia.

A local security official and a battalion commander met with U.S. diplomats three days before the attack and warned the Americans about deteriorating security in the area.

Ambassador Stevens' diary, which was later found at the compound, recorded his concern about the growing al-Qaeda presence in the area and his worry about being on an al-Qaeda hit list. Additional security was requested for the mission in Benghazi but was denied by Charlene Lamb at the U.S. State Department. They were desiring to project an image of normalcy.

Clinton initially accepted the responsibility for the failure to provide additional security but subsequently back-tracked. She now claimed, the specific security requests pertaining to Benghazi ... were handled by the security professionals in the State Department, "I didn't see those requests, I didn't approve them, I didn't deny them."

(U.S. Ambassador Chris Stevens)

Clinton, Obama, and many government officials tried to cover up the fact that this was a terrorist attack and touted a story that the attack was a spontaneous reaction to an obscure YouTube video titled the Innocence of Muslims. The maker of the obscure video was arrested by federal officials despite there being no connection between his video and the attack. He remained held on separate charges that he violated his probation by using a pseudonym in making the film. After a great deal of pressure, Clinton, Obama, and other government officials changed their story and labeled Benghazi as a terrorist attack and unrelated to the YouTube video.

It's important to note that as the event was occurring in Benghazi, Clinton sent a message to her daughter Chelsea, via the unsecured server, and stated that a terrorist attack was currently occurring in Benghazi. There was no mention of a spontaneous protest nor a connection to the YouTube video. Spectators on the ground also confirmed that there were not protests prior to the terrorist attack on the consulate.

It's hard to decide if the actual attack or the attempt to cover it up was more detrimental to the victims and their families. The families need closure and they were denied it. The families wanted the truth and tried to get it from Clinton. The truth has yet to come out.

According Saxena, V., 2015, "Democrat presidential candidate and former Secretary of State Hillary Clinton mercilessly threw the families of Benghazi victims Chris Stevens, Sean Smith, Glen Doherty and Tyrone Woods under the bus in a bid to divert blame away from her own despicable subversion of the truth. "I can't help it if the people think there has to be something else," Clinton replied when asked why she misled the victims' families by blaming the 2012 Benghazi attack on an Internet trailer of an anti-Islamic movie. She went on to cite the "fog of war" for causing a mix-up of information, then claimed that she did not discover the actual truth, that the attack occurred as part of a terrorist plot, by the next morning." Hillary Clinton's e-mail to her daughter Chelsea shows she knew this was a terrorist attack. She was lying to the families of the victims.

The cover up may or may not be of Clinton's making. It appears that Obama may have played a greater role. All the video footage covering the attack was retrieved and should have been able to provide some answers, but it was deemed top secret and locked away even from members of congress involved in the investigation. One additional reason the videos may be kept secret involves multiple reports supporting that the Ambassador was sodomize, tortured and castrated prior to being murdered and dragged naked through the streets.

The reason additional security was not provided, why military planes were not sent in and why the story has been covered up is currently speculation. Evidence suggests that the CIA annex was being used to smuggle weapons to "moderate" forces in Libya and that many of those weapons ended up on the hands of Al Qaeda. If this is true it is possible that the weapons used in the attack were American. If the videos were released the weapons would be identified as American and jeopardize the covert CIA mission.

There is also evidence that weapons deals were made through the Qatari government to supply "moderates" in Syria wishing to overthrow Assad. Those "moderates" morphed into the group now known as ISIS. This is what the Russians have contended and would also explain the almost instantaneous rise of this new, major terrorist group. Turkey and Russia have separately accused the United States of backing terrorist groups in Syria. Turkish President Erdogan said that he had evidence that US-led coalition forces gave support to ISIS.

The investigation concluded with few questions answered. Many of the needed documents were never provided to the committee.

According to Bunker, Theodore, 2016, committee member "Pompeo criticized the report for not faulting former Secretary of State Hillary Clinton, and released a supplement, concluding that Clinton failed to lead as the head of the State Department, and that the administration misled the public about the attack in Benghazi.

It is important to note that some of the newly discovered Clinton E-mails which she did not turned over to the FBI are related to conversations about Benghazi.

THE IMPACT ON NOT LOCKING HER UP

Under the Obama administration the departmental entities that we have trusted for generations have become politicized and thus compromised. Their scandals have been exposed and the public's trust has been eroded.

Faith in the integrity of these institutions must be built before any documents or witnesses from these departments would be considered credible by all. Any defense attorney who is faced with a difficult case will do his or her best to erode the credibility of the oppositions witnesses. In today's conditions, those witnesses would not hold up to scrutiny.

If the prosecution were successful in providing appropriate documentation and witnesses, there is always the chance that a case of this magnitude would expose additional scandal, negligence, and incompetence within the individual departments.

It is important that time be dedicated to regaining public opinion that these departments are not scandal free, both for the success of the prosecution and the success of the country moving forward.

IMPACT OF CURRENT WORLD EVENTS

There are multiple hot spots in our world right now; places where war can erupt at any time. We must remain vigilant, seize opportunities for diplomacy and plan for the worst-case scenarios. A major prosecution case, involving a politician and possibly implicating our government departments would be a huge distraction and perhaps even direct resources and sway political alliances away from focusing on protecting our country.

North Korea

In the past it was easy to laugh off North Korea's empty threats. A nuclear armed North Korea is a different story. The U.S. knows North Korea has nuclear weapons, satellites, and missiles. It is unlikely either side will initiate a war without provocation. It is difficult to determine what form that provocation may take and worrisome that a false flag event could be staged by either party, or worse a third-party intent on forcing the United States into a war.

Missiles are not the biggest concern since North Korea is not yet at the technological stage to hit the U.S. mainland and any launch would likely be a single missile which the American military can shoot down. The biggest concern should be submarines.

North Korea has around 90 known submarines. In the recent past, they were mostly older, retired soviet submarines which the U.S. Navy could easily track by their noise. The North stole submarine construction plans from South Korea and are now mass-producing their own, more advanced submarines. They are not so easy to track.

North Korea does not have the ability to launch from a submarine, and sea launches are not a current concern. They could, however, load nuclear weapons onto the submarines, hide their travels by shadowing beneath cargo ships and enter our ports, particularly Seattle, San Francisco, and Los Angeles. The North Korean crews need not be aware that they are on a kamikaze mission. Only willing commanders would be aware of the mission, surface the sub and detonate the nuclear weapon. If they chose not to detonate, the subs could be used as insurance policy so that the U.S. doesn't invade North Korea or a means to blackmail the United States into lifting sanctions.

Any war with North Korea would certainly be won by the United States but at a very high cost to both sides. It is also important to note that as the tensions grew in the region, U.S. arms sales to our allies in the region skyrocketed.

Russia

Russian annexation of the Crimea resulted in the relationship between the United States and Russia dissolving into a state comparable if not worse than during the cold war. Obama placed and coerced others to place sanctions on Russia. Sanctions are only effective if there is a demand that must be met for sanctions to be lifted. No demands were made. President Trump is powerless to rebuild relationships with Russia as long as the warrantless Russia collusion investigation is going on; in fact, congress has assumed power over lifting sanctions until the collusion investigation ends.

The Crimea is home to the Russian Black Sea fleet. The majority of people living in Crimea are Russian nationals. It was historically Russian but was given as a gift to Ukraine under soviet rule, while there was no concept that the USSR would ever break up. When American press polled people in Crimea they discovered that 90% of those living in Crimea supported Russian annexation. The Crimea is of strategic and National Security interest to Russia.

(Viktor Yanukovych)

In 2014 the Ukraine had a revolution. The revolution was caused by mixed desires of the people to either become more closely aligned the European Union or strengthen ties with Russia. Each choice was tied to a large influx of financial support from whichever side was chosen. Duly elected President Yanukovych sided with Russia but was summarily overthrown and fled to Russia. Russia has claimed the U.S. influenced the revolution and while no U.S. troops were present, 300 or more blackwater mercenary soldiers were known to be in the Ukraine.

Russia responded with sanctions of its own. They also turned to markets in Asia and demonstrated their frustration through increased showcasing of their military might. Their military provocations resulted in U.S. weapons sales to Europe skyrocketing.

Ukrainian lawmaker Artemenko came up with a creative solution to the current situation. He proposed that the Crimea be leased to Russia for 50 to 100 years, thus ending the current stalemate. Obama ignored the opportunity. Artemenko is currently presenting the plan to the Trump administration.

Russia will never likely be a true ally of the United States, but with improved relations, it certainly can be a cooperative partner in solving many of the worlds regional problems. It is not in our country's best interest to isolate and ostracize Russia.

Syria

Syria is a satellite state of Russia and U.S. intervention in Syria has always been prevented by a lack of desire to provoke Russia. When ISIS took route in Syria and Iraq it appeared suddenly and drew the condemnation of the world due to its horrific torture, often caught on video. It was difficult to understand how this group came to be as quickly as it did.

Powerless to defend itself, Syria welcomes any country willing to help fight ISIS, including the U.S. In time, Syria and Russia analyzed the actions of the U.S. military under Obama and realized U.S. actions had little effect on ISIS but was devastating the vital infrastructure of the Assad regime, thus bolstering ISIS. Turkey also claimed the U.S. and its allies (particularly Qatar) were supporting ISIS through arms sales. These contentions were likely true under the Obama administration. The covert mission must not have been conveyed to President Trump, who has made huge strides in fighting ISIS since taking office.

Syria is a pawn, being used by Russia and the U.S. Both countries want to build pipelines through Syria. The Russian pipeline is determinant upon Assad staying in power or improving relations with Turkey. Russia has been improving those relationships while slowly eroding the relationship between Turkey and western governments. Russia has since garnered majority control of Kazakhstan's oil and as relations improve with Turkey, the propose pipeline has moved north to Turkey.

Qatar also wants to build a pipeline across Syria. A Qatari pipeline is determinant upon the overthrow of the Assad government. The grand plan was for ISIS to overthrow Assad and then for the U.S. to overthrow ISIS.

Tensions in the region have been high with new provocations involving Iran, Saudi Arabia, Yemen, United Arab Emirates and Israel. U.S. weapons sales to this region have skyrocketed during the crisis.

China

Since Bill Clinton granted free trade status to China, the two countries have become symbiotic. China needs the U.S. to sustain its new-found wealth and due to factories closing in the U.S., America is reliant on China for many goods, including parts necessary for America's military.

As China's wealth grew, they invested in infrastructure and military advancements. They have also become more involved in international affairs through investments particularly in Africa and South America. Venezuela, which is near financial collapse, is heavily indebted to China. It has been reported that Venezuela even offered China one of their islands as debt payment. China also holds a large amount of U.S. debt in the form of treasury bonds.

China wants to be a regional power if not a world power. They have claimed all of the South China Sea and created man-made islands that have transformed into military bases. The U.S. has boldly challenged China's claim. The U.S. has strong allies in the region which include, Japan, South Korea, and the Philippines. In order to be a regional power, China must erode U.S. influence in the region. When it comes to North Korea, China is in a tenuous position. While financially it is dependent on good relations with the U.S., it does not want U.S. military presence in the region to grow in strength and support. Sales of U.S. weapons in the region have skyrocketed since China has flexed its military muscle and vocalized its intention to control the South China Sea.

(Xi Jinping)

THE IMPACT ON NOT LOCKING HER UP

Successfully preventing a war requires government unity. Successfully engaging in war requires government unity.

A prolonged prosecution would be divisive. Despite the evidence, it would likely be seen by some as a political witch hunt. Members of congress may politicize the investigation and vote against necessary military appropriations in retaliation. Secrets that may be unveiled during trial could damage our relationships with key allies or threaten morale within our own military.

Successful prosecution of Clinton would be much more probable once one or more of the current international crisis's is resolved.

THE
PUPPET
MASTERS

There are wealthy and powerful individuals throughout our world who yield those resources to influence others. Some are familiar to us such as George Soros who funds a vast network of liberal organizations throughout the world, or the Koch brothers who fund vast ultra-conservative organizations throughout the world.

(George Soros)

Puppet masters can influence what the public knows, what the public thinks, what is kept from the public as well as influence public officials through deep pocketed campaign donations.

According to Robertson, Steve, 2017, *In this day and age of vast amounts of news and media that bombard and compete for public attention fewer and fewer are able to discriminate fact from fiction. Shocking tabloid headlines, once reserved for amusement at grocery store line checkout, are now used by the mainstream press to bait the hook to get the consumer to bite and read/watch more. Journalists and reporters, if you can now call them such, are woefully compromised in the bias they take in propagandizing issues that ultimately serve the agenda of the media giants and hidden elite (owners of these media conglomerates) for whom they work and shape the perceptional lens of the masses.*

One of the greatest known masterminds of media propaganda and tactical distraction was the late Dr. Edward L. Bernays. He was considered the founding Father of Public Relations and was also the nephew of Sigmund Freud.

(Edward Bernays)

Bernays' agenda of herding society in specific directions, on behalf of those who envisioned a new world order, is apparent in his quote: "We are governed, our minds are molded, our tastes formed, our ideas suggested, largely by men we have never heard of... If we understand the mechanism and motives of the group mind, it is now possible to control and regiment the masses according to our will without them knowing it...The conscious and intellectual manipulation of the organized habits and opinions of the masses is an important element in democratic society. Those who manipulate this unseen mechanism of society constitute an invisible government which is the true ruling power of our country."

In order to place the agenda and motive of mind-controlling society through the modern media machine, consider a few historic quotes that point to people behind such actions.

"All Wars are fought for money" – Socrates "When one with honeyed words but evil mind persuades the mob, great woes befall the state." — Euripides

The means of defense against foreign danger have been always the instruments of tyranny at home. Among the Romans it was a standing maxim to excite a war, whenever a revolt was apprehended. Throughout all Europe, the armies kept up under the pretext of defending, have enslaved the people." — James Madison

"Experience has shown, that even under the best forms of government those entrusted with power have, in time, and by slow operations, perverted it into tyranny." — Thomas Jefferson

"Those who would give up essential liberty to purchase a little temporary safety, deserve neither liberty or safety." – Benjamin Franklin

"In every age it has been the tyrant, the oppressor and the exploiter who has wrapped himself in the cloak of patriotism, or religion, or both to deceive and overawe the People." — Eugene Victor Debs,

"Those who are capable of tyranny are capable of perjury to sustain it." — Lysander Spooner"

One of the greatest truisms of the human existence and wisdom, when describing the various monstrous realities that have occurred on our earth, is "Follow the money."

Puppet masters control the political elite of both parties in the United States. Many well-established politicians are beholding to these powerful people and are more than willing to push legislation conceived in the controller's best interests. The puppet masters on both sides do not like President Trump because he is an outsider who they cannot yet control.

THE IMPACT ON NOT LOCKING HER UP

Given that puppet masters on both sides of the political spectrum dislike President Trump there is a high likelihood that they would try to disrupt proceedings. They could call upon politicians loyal to them, introduce bogus evidence to overwhelm, discredit or bury true evidence, feed false news to the media, pay for demonstrations, and incite violence.

WE

ARE

NOT

DESPOTS

Never dismiss Hillary Clinton. She is as brilliant as she is corrupt. She knows how the political game is played and is well aware of the factors mentioned in this book. She knows the risks to our country, our government, our people and our integrity on the international stage if she is prosecuted. She is also aware of her own vulnerabilities although she is an accomplished poker player and bluffing comes as naturally to her as her other lies.

> According to Delk, Josh, 2017, *Hillary Clinton warned that if President Trump directs his Justice Department to investigate her role in a 2010 sale of a uranium company, it would be "a disastrous step into politicizing the Justice Department.This is such an abuse of power," that the Justice Department is considering appointing a special counsel to investigate, said Clinton.*

A typical propaganda practice on the Nazi's was to loudly blame others for things you are actually doing. Under Holder and Lynch the Department of Justice (DOJ) became a political tool for Obama and Clinton. It had never been more politicized to block or punish anyone who threatened the administration. Clinton is using deflection by proactively making this charge against the current DOJ.

Clinton is correct that the Uranium One deal will probably not result in a conviction. Too many others were involved, and the deal itself is not well understood by most people. The U.S. portion of the deal was just a bonus to a much bigger deal with Uranium One in Kazakhstan. The U.S. and Canadian Uranium was to be processed here by the Russians and sold back to America, it was not to leave. This was combined with a deal to allow Russia access to help build energy infrastructure in the U.S.

The only compelling aspects of Uranium One is Obama's western land grab in the name of creating national monuments, and the money that filtered into the Clinton Foundation. A more effective case would be to focus on the Clinton Foundation with Uranium One as an ancillary component.

(Delk cont.)"I regret if they do it because it will be such a disastrous step to politicizing the justice system," she said. "If they send a signal that we're going to be like some dictatorship, like some authoritarian regime, where political opponents are going to be unfairly, fraudulently investigated, that rips at the fabric of the contract we have, that we can trust our justice system."

Hillary Clinton is 100% correct in this assessment, particularly since she made the claim now, prior to any indictment. She is well versed at playing the victim, and if she can garner any international attention by claiming she is being persecuted politically at this juncture, it is to her advantage.

It is a universally condemned practice that when dictators come to power, they purge the country of political opponents. She could make the case that prosecuting her is tantamount. Some people in the United Nations would certainly seize upon the opportunity to denigrate the United States. The true difference is she is not a political threat to anyone, she is a criminal trying to avoid paying for her crimes.

(Delk cont.) Clinton said she is "not concerned" with whether a special counsel will be appointed or that she will face indictments "because I know that there

is no basis to it. And at the end of the day, nothing will come of it, but it will, you know, cause a lot of terrible consequences that we might live with for a really long time," she said

Here she is bluffing. She can only be terrified. Had she been elected all her criminal deeds would have been buried. She lost, and those crimes are being exposed. Loyalists are distancing themselves, abandoning her or throwing her under the bus.

(Hillary Clinton)

THE ROLE OF ATTORNEY GENERAL

Many American's voted for Donald Trump because they were tired of the establishment ignoring the crimes of the elite. The mantra, "Lock her up" gave hope that justice would be served, and Clinton would be held accountable for her crimes at last. Prosecuting her is not a simple matter and if it is to occur, the timing and condition must be right.

(Jeff Sessions)

According to McCarthy, Andrew, 2016, *The Attorney General can decline prosecution, which the executive branch has the unreviewable constitutional power to do, regardless of how damning the proof of crimes might be. Just as no law may compel the Justice Department to prosecute a case, there is also no law that requires the Attorney General to decide whether to prosecute within a specific period of time, much less to explain a decision not to prosecute.*

The FBI have no power to force the Justice Department to prosecute; it has no power to force the Justice Department to decide whether to prosecute. The Obama Justice Department, during Eric Holder's tenure and continuing into Ms. Lynch's stewardship, has been the most politicized in American history. It is often observed that, in using the executive's law-enforcement powers against the administration's adversaries, the real weapon is the process, not the ability to trump up charges and make them stick. The Justice Department's stable of community organizers and "social justice" crusaders know that persons, organizations, and companies can be ruined by the mere threat of an indictment even if one is never forthcoming. "Suspects" can be financially bankrupted and emotionally wrecked by the incessant demands for documentary information, interviews by federal agents, requests for grand-jury testimony, and so on. The Justice Department can stretch the vexatious process out for years. Innocent people can be pressured to plead guilty, just as innocent businesses and even municipal police departments can be browbeaten into signing intrusive settlements just to get the unbearable, prohibitively expensive process over with.

No matter how much media and public interest there is in the progress of an investigation, prosecutors can always say that grand-jury secrecy rules and the integrity of the evidence-gathering process dictate that the Justice Department make no public comment while potential charges are being considered.

Jeff Sessions is under no obligation to pursue a prosecution. He also is under no time limit to decide on the matter. Waiting until confidence in government agencies is restored is wise. Waiting until people who were embedded into agencies by prior presidents are identified and possibly removed is wise. Waiting until the fury of the left that followed the election lessens is wise. Waiting to see if Clinton's political allies distance themselves is wise. Waiting to see if her political allies turn against her for manipulating the DNC is wise. Waiting to collect and assess untainted evidence is wise.

Ironically, one of the reasons Sessions must distance himself, or recuse himself, at the moment, is the very reason he was appointed by Donald Trump. Donald Trump's rallying cry throughout the election was "lock her up", and many of us agreed. Trump's appointment of Sessions was seen by most of us as the means to accomplish this mission but in fact has tied Session's hands, at least for the moment. His prosecution of Clinton must be seen as apolitical in order to succeed.

Our own assumption of her guilt, including the President's is causing the delay in justice we all hope for. Clinton has committed crimes that deserve to be punished. The question is, what price are we willing to endure as a country in order to bring her to justice?

Perhaps the point we all must be thankful for is we dodged a bullet by not electing her and perhaps that is all the justice we will get.

Bibliography

Anderson, Lisa. "Demystifying the Arab Spring." Foreign
Affairs, Council on Foreign Relations, 2011

Boehm, Ken. "IRS Scandal: America Needs the Truth."
CNN, Cable News Network, 4 Sept. 2013

Bolger, Nick. "Report: Education Dept. Official Received
Secret Bonuses Despite Losing Billions to Fraud,
Corruption." Washington Free Beacon, 2 June 2017

Bunker, Theodore. "Benghazi Congressional Investigation
Officially Over With Final Report." Newsmax.
Independent American, 9 Sept. 2016

Delk, Josh. "Clinton: DOJ Investigating Me Would Be
'Abuse of Power'." The Hill, MSN, 15 Nov. 2017

Ditz, Jason. "Glaspie Memo Leaked: US Dealings With
Iraq Ahead of 1990 Invasion of Kuwait Detailed."
News From Antiwar.com, 24 Jan. 2011

Fishel, Justin. "Hillary Clinton's Long-Awaited Benghazi
Hearing Marked by Testy Exchanges." ABC News.
ABC News Network, 22 Oct. 2015

Greenwood, Max. "Rand Paul Assaulted at Kentucky
Home: Police." The Hill, 4 Nov. 2017

Jones, Ed. "China Killed or Jailed up to 20 US Spies in
2010-12: Report." Agence France Presse, AFP, 21
May 2017

Leigh, David. "US Embassy Cables Leak Sparks Global
Diplomatic Crisis." The Guardian, 2010

Marshall, Andrew. "Empire Under Obama: America's "Secret Wars" in Over 100 Countries Around the World." Truthout, 2013

McCarthy, Andrew C. "The Justice Department's Hillary Stonewall." National Review, 29 Mar. 2016

Ray, Ellen. "U.S. Military and Corporate Recolonization of the Congo." Congo U.S. Military and Corporate Recolonization of the Congo, Covert Action Quarterly, 2000

Robertson, Steve. "Puppet Masters of Media Propaganda." Veterans Today, 20 Oct. 2017

Rosiak, Luke. "Obama Appointees Must Repay Salaries After Enabling Fraud." The Daily Caller, The Daily Caller, 7 Apr. 2016

Savage, Charlie. "Sex, Drug Use and Graft Cited in Interior Department." The New York Times, The New York Times, 10 Sept. 2008

Saxena, V. "SICK: Hillary Clinton Calls Out Families of Benghazi Victims as LIARS on Live TV." Conservative Tribune., 11 Dec. 2015

Shear, Michael, et al. "Steve Scalise Among 4 Shot at Baseball Field; Suspect Is Dead." The New York Times, The New York Times, 14 June 2017

Westby, Jody. "It Is A Scandal That No One Is Investigating the NSA." Forbes, Forbes Magazine, 1 Feb. 2014

Wyler, Grace. "Here's What You Need To Know About The Gun Running Scandal That Could Destroy

Obama's Attorney General." Business Insider,
Business Insider, 20 June 2012